I0114756

# YOUR
*Neurodiverse*
## CHILD

# YOUR
# Neurodiverse
# CHILD

## How to Help Kids with Learning, Attention, and Neurocognitive Challenges Thrive

## NECHAMA SORSCHER

ROWMAN & LITTLEFIELD
Lanham • Boulder • New York • London

Published by Rowman & Littlefield
An imprint of The Rowman & Littlefield Publishing Group, Inc.
4501 Forbes Boulevard, Suite 200, Lanham, Maryland 20706
www.rowman.com

86-90 Paul Street, London EC2A 4NE, United Kingdom

Copyright © 2025 by Nechama Sorscher

*All rights reserved.* No part of this book may be reproduced in any form or by any electronic or mechanical means, including information storage and retrieval systems, without written permission from the publisher, except by a reviewer who may quote passages in a review.

British Library Cataloguing in Publication Information Available

Library of Congress Cataloging-in-Publication Data Available

ISBN 978-1-5381-9213-9 (cloth) | ISBN 978-1-5381-9214-6 (ebook)

To my three wonderful children,
Joshua, Nathan, and Rachel.
Thank you for teaching me, inspiring me,
and celebrating our family—with all its ups and downs.

# CONTENTS

# ACKNOWLEDGMENTS

I'd like to gratefully acknowledge the parents and teachers with whom I have had the privilege to consult and who have entrusted their children to me. You are on the front lines, and I have nothing but respect and admiration for your thoughtfulness and commitment to your children.

Thank you to my wonderful editor and friend Jill Harris—for her meticulous reading and help with fleshing out my ideas; to my tireless assistant Alexander Celia, who is always up for chasing down references and proofreading for typos; to my parents Esther and Yehuda Sorscher, for their encouragement and support; to my partner, Farnoush Safavi, for her belief in me and for her availability for brainstorming; and, lastly, to my mentor, Dr. Clarice Kestenbaum, for always being there and having full confidence in me.

# WHAT ARE ATTENTION DEFICIT DISORDER AND LEARNING DISORDERS AND HOW TO IDENTIFY THEM IN YOUR CHILD

What are neurocognitive challenges? This chapter helps you begin to understand the difficulties your child is facing and prepare a road map for his or her success. Sadly, almost half of parents believe incorrectly that children will outgrow attention deficit disorder (ADD) and learning disorders (LD), and, shockingly, 33 percent of educators report that what sometimes is called a learning disorder is really just laziness.[1] Understanding your child's neurodivergence is the solution to helping your child cope with challenges and flourish academically, socially, and emotionally.

Attention and learning disorders are neurocognitive impairments. Although we still don't know enough about how the neurodivergent brain works, we can conceptualize it as faulty signaling between the brain and the body. It's similar to when you're tired and your brain doesn't work as quickly or efficiently as usual. In fact, one hypothesis is that people with ADD have sleep disturbances and high slow-wave sleep activity in their brain.[2] Although we all have brain waves that are operating in our brains at all times, people with ADD produce an inordinate number of sleep waves. Thus, they devote a lot of their energy to waking up their brain. It's similar to when you are driving a car and you feel sleepy; you roll down the windows, put the music on loudly, tap your fingers on the steering wheel—anything to help yourself stay alert. That's what people with ADD do when they fidget, pace, and multitask, all behaviors that can be viewed as their attempts to stimulate a sleepy brain.

People with LD perceive the world differently because the part of their brain responsible for processing information is underdeveloped.

If you have ever heard the saying, "garbage in, garbage out," you can imagine that receiving faulty information from your eyes or ears compromises your ability to respond correctly. This is what happens with neurodivergent children; the signals in their brain get crossed, making it anywhere from difficult to nearly impossible to concentrate, learn certain things, or navigate social situations smoothly. Happily, with understanding, patience, and a strategic approach that you will learn in this book, you can significantly help your child cope with these challenges and even flourish using their unique skills and talents. But on the path to success, these issues can have tremendous psychological and emotional impact, the burden of which is often as challenging as the presentation of the problem itself. As a clinician, parent, or teacher, unraveling these complexities is like exploring a maze. Let's first take a look at ADD and what's called language-based LD.

## ATTENTION DEFICIT DISORDER (ADD)

ADD is seen across a wide spectrum from mild to severe and pertains to difficulties with focus, impulsivity, and hyperactivity. You might notice your child displays a sort of "jumpiness," a general sense of being unable to sit still, even acting on impulse without thinking. Others can have specific motor and sensory-seeking activities such as fidgeting or jiggling. You've watched those characters in a movie or TV show who are hyper-focused on one thing, bouncing from idea to idea, or sometimes simply forgetting what they were doing a minute ago. Some people may see this in the well-known character Ferris Bueller from the movie *Ferris Bueller's Day Off*. A high school student who is notorious for his charming antics, clever escapes, and ability to seize the moment, Ferris is always bounding from one idea to another. He is constantly on the mischievous move and seemingly unaware of the consequences of his actions. Though it's never explicitly stated that he has ADD, some of his behavior demonstrates the same hyperactivity, impulsivity, and traits associated with the condition. Of course, it's important to note that fictional characters are often exaggerated for entertainment, but they can be relatable examples, showing that ADD can also have the gift of a brain energized to explore the universe with a different kind of curiosity, an out-of-the-box thinking that can see connections others might miss. With the right support, these character traits can be channeled to do extraordinary things.

The weightier side of ADD has other students appear inattentive, spacey, or dreamy. We all know those kids who can't seem to remember where they put their shoes or phone or are unable to organize their papers. Their backpacks look more like a tornado of disorganized mess, and they may have difficulty initiating or following up with plans or being on time. They often end up feeling frustrated, overwhelmed, and, critically, bad about themselves.

The social, or apparent antisocial, aspect of ADD can be tremendously isolating. Imagine feeling like you're drifting in a world that moves at a different pace. Behind the spaciness and the distant gazes lies a struggle to focus on the tasks and conversations around them. Simply remembering where they put their belongings can turn into an hours-long search, causing them to withdraw and appear antisocial. Zoning out in the middle of conversations can make them feel disconnected from their peers, further adding to their sense of loneliness. Among these students, impulsivity can be a very real issue, causing them to interrupt others without intending to be rude. This kind of behavior combined with a need to be the center of attention can lead to strained relationships or no relationships at all, as their peers don't have the knowledge, interest, or empathy to understand such struggles.

ADD is tightly linked to something known as executive function disorder. Executive functioning is what gives us the ability to successfully engage in goal-directed action. It's what allows us to control our behavior, prepare for future events, and, ultimately, achieve goals. It's all part of planning, focusing attention, remembering instructions, and managing multiple tasks. Students with poor executive functioning have trouble organizing, keeping track of time and appointments, processing information efficiently, and remembering details. They're often disorganized, can't keep track of their schedule, forget important information, misplace items, and—to the chagrin of parents and teachers—are generally quite messy. Children with ADD often fatigue easily because they expend so much energy trying to focus. Unlike people without ADD, concentration itself puts extraordinary demand on their systems. If you can, imagine people without ADD as having a smartphone as a brain, an advanced model with a battery that lasts all day without much effort. But those with ADD have a different battery that needs constant charging. Concentration becomes an energy-hungry app that keeps running in the background, sapping the battery life rapidly. They have to constantly recharge and manage their energy levels just to keep up with the demands of focusing. They find it difficult to complete assignments and are frequently mislabeled as "lazy, careless, and thoughtless." The extra effort they have to make for even seemingly simple tasks can be like running multiple power-hungry apps on their smartphone simultaneously. No wonder they fatigue so easily! Understanding this analogy helps us to see that these children are not being lazy or indifferent. Far from it, they're dealing with a unique system that requires special attention and understanding.

Socially, children with ADD can have trouble sustaining friendships and following conversations as they tend to lose focus, "space out," and become distracted. This absent-mindedness and tendency to go off on tangents in conversation makes them appear unempathetic or insensitive as friends. People who suffer from organizational difficulties are also greatly hampered in their ability to navigate the logistics of social events, as they have trouble planning and following through on get-togethers. They are often late to events and have significant time management issues causing their family, friends, teachers, and bosses to erroneously conclude that they "don't care," are not prioritizing the event or task, or simply not exerting sufficient effort. People with ADD can forget entirely to show up at a mutually agreed-upon time, inadvertently stranding a friend who will then be reluctant to reschedule due to what he or she interprets as "flakiness." We can understand this need to be the center of attention as an extension of getting stimulation from the environment; it is similar to listening to loud music as a "pick-me-up." Getting attention from peers and adults functions as a centering experience for the restless brain with which these children are contending. Let's consider how ADD impairs social skills with this example of a patient of mine.

Marcie, a bubbly, energetic fourteen-year-old girl, consulted with me due to experiences of painful social rejections. I quickly picked up on a pattern in her social life: Marcie easily would make friends with other

girls; she initially would be included in the group and start to feel comfortable socially. But just as she gained social traction, the girls would,
bewilderingly, retreat. They no longer included her in their outings,
leaving her feeling rejected and hurt and forcing her to pursue other
social opportunities. As I began to make sense of this tangled social
web of Marcie's experiences, it became clear that Marcie inadvertently
behaved in ways that were off-putting to her peers. For example, she was
consistently the last person to get on the bus after volleyball practice
and often needed to have the whole team wait for her as she ran off the
bus in search of something—her sweatshirt or backpack that she left
behind. Sometimes she blurted out indiscreet comments and observations about other students or teachers without confirming that her peers
shared these views. "Wow, this outfit is so ugly," Marcie stage-whispered
to a peer about her friend's dress. In this way, her ADD and her behavior
made her appear strange, placing her in an isolated box.

A distinction within the ADD spectrum is those with inattentive
versus hyperactive ADD. People with inattentive ADD tend to be
spacey and dreamy, marked by a quiet withdrawal from tasks. This sort
of "spacing out" can manifest as staring, seemingly aimlessly, out the
window, doodling, and daydreaming. Inattentive children often miss information and thus have difficulty performing well as a result. In contrast,
those with hyperactive ADD are impulsive with poor self-regulation.
In a school setting, a common manifestation of hyperactive ADD is
to become the "class clown," disrupting lessons due to impulsivity. In
addition, these children get easily frustrated by challenges and instead
of persevering on tasks, they may try to distract themselves and others
by chatting, making jokes, and wandering around the classroom. Poor
impulse control stems from a deficit in the inhibitory mechanisms of
the brain. In other words, people with ADD simply do not have access
to the part of the brain that tells us to "look before you leap." Thus, they
rush to act or blurt out a comment that is, at best, misunderstood or, at
worst, gets them in trouble. This impulsivity also hinders their ability to
relate to peers, as they may utter something insulting. Individuals with
hyperactive ADD can also lack the attention span to listen both in social
conversations or in the classroom, with younger children struggling to
sit and listen to a simple library story.

Life can be very difficult for people with ADD. Notably, of equal importance are the reactions to such behavior from peers, teachers, and parents. These almost always turn into messages and labels that become internalized, the painful result of which is that the person with ADD ends up creating a personal narrative in which he or she is bad, lazy, stupid, or just a dreamer. The psychological consequences are deeply upsetting and long lasting and include low self-esteem, shame, isolation, anxiety, and depression.

Noah was a delightful patient of mine, a serious eight-year-old boy who enjoys reading, math, and socializing with his friends. However, he experienced significant stress and anxiety both in school and at home because he had great difficulty doing his homework. In fact, because he frequently forgot that he even had homework, he would neglect to complete his assignments entirely. And if he did manage to remember to do his homework, he would simply forget to hand it in! Still, his inherent intelligence and curiosity allowed him to enjoy participating in class and he was able to impress his teacher with his insight and analysis. But his strengths were hampered by the fact that his backpack and desk were messy and disorganized, causing him difficulty in accessing his assignments and submitting them on time. These habits made it seem as if he was a careless, thoughtless student who was lazy and didn't apply himself. When criticized for his habits, Noah became more anxious and then withdrew from his homework, creating the self-fulfilling prophecy that he didn't care about his schoolwork. Most telling was his teacher's observation that Noah would misplace a piece of paper just moments after handing it to him. She said, "I would give it to him as he passed my desk and at some point, during the time it took him to walk from the desk back to his seat, the paper magically vanished!" Not surprisingly, when I tested Noah, the results revealed a diagnosis of ADD, inattentive type.

As we saw with the example of Ferris Bueller, it's important to note that there are extremely positive aspects of ADD. Individuals with ADD are often uniquely poised to navigate our current culture, because their attention span is quite flexible. They are able to "hyper-focus" on tasks that catch their interest and can happily spend hours on creative pursuits, computer programming, or other areas where their passions are cultivated to bloom. They also tend to retain a childlike playfulness, spontaneity, imagination, and sense of wonder. These qualities are essential to many creative and scientific pursuits. People with ADD have extraordinarily high levels of energy and what's called a "roaming" quality of attention, in which they can notice and take in several details simultaneously. In addition, they can focus intensely for short bursts of time. You can think of attention as a flashlight with multiple settings. First it's on the brightest, most intense light and, then suddenly, it starts to blink on and off, all the while sweeping the room and capturing multiple images. People with ADD have this capacity and their high energy level contributes to productivity and the ability to juggle tasks. They naturally excel as entrepreneurs, salespeople, inventors, artists, and fitness instructors. This is a reminder to parents and teachers to understand that those with ADD have unique and gifted minds and to continually focus on those strengths. Most importantly, recognizing the positive qualities of ADD helps us create a positive narrative that we can convey to our children, improving their confidence and appreciation of themselves.

## LEARNING DISABILITIES (LD)

In my practice I see a wide range of neurocognitive challenges, many with their own unique powers and their own unique quirks. Some difficulties are more challenging than others, but they all form a fantastic tapestry of human diversity and potential. We have learned thus far about ADD and ADHD. Along the neurodivergent experience is learning disorders, or disabilities, which is a comprehensive category for a wide range of specific learning challenges that can make reading, writing, spelling, and math hard for students. LD can also impact the way a student organizes or recalls, hears, speaks, and remembers information. As a first step, it is essential for students, parents, and educators to understand that learning issues have absolutely nothing to do with intelligence, hearing, or vision issues. In fact, people with LD often have average or above-average intelligence. Yet, there is a discrepancy between their achievements and their potential, wherein they notably underachieve academically. In the field of neuropsychology, we refer to the deficits in LD as select, meaning specific, not global. Because LD manifests in cognitive weaknesses across basic academic skills, language development, and attention and memory, findings on neuropsychological and neuroeducational evaluations can, confusingly, range from "very superior" to "deficient." For those with LD, it's as if they experience a puzzling malfunction in one area while they can do other tasks very easily. For example, many people with LD are excellent readers but consistently fail every math test. These challenges can be really confusing and anxiety producing. Adding to the pain of the experience is that they are often misunderstood, and misdiagnosed, both by the individuals themselves and by others. Sadly, in order to process and understand what could be going on, a false narrative that the student is being lazy, bad, stupid, and/or unmotivated is created as an alternative explanation.

Children with language-based learning disorders show up with relatively weak language skills and stronger visual-spatial skills. These students frequently have difficulty with reading and writing, and typically perform better on subjects such as math and science. Academic challenges may include difficulty following directions, understanding lectures, and taking notes. Compared to their peers, they simply can't keep up. Children with language-based learning disorders can complain of being "tongue tied." They're not so good at engaging in witty and playful conversations or even initiating or sustaining conversation, so they're truly at a significant social disadvantage.

My patient, Michael, a sweet and polite high schooler, expressed that he feels lost during lunch with his peers. He explained, "I can't find the words to keep up with my friends. They say I'm quiet and shy, but the conversation goes too quickly for me." Unfortunately, these children are often mislabeled as "oppositional" or "resistant" due to their compromised expressive language skills. Understandably for these students, anxiety quickly rises to the surface because they are often criticized for what others perceive as their unwillingness to participate. Another student, Laura, was issued report cards with teachers labeling her as "nonparticipatory" along with comments that she "does not raise her hand," "doesn't respond when called upon," "looks down at her desk instead of looking at the teacher." Laura tearfully expressed that being called upon in class was "torture," because her words failed her and her mind went blank.

Language-based learning disabilities fall into two categories: expressive and receptive. But before we dive into them, let's talk for a moment about language processing in general, where an intricate dance of words and communication takes center stage. The dance begins with language processing, where the brain's left hemisphere—in the temporal and frontal lobes—plays an important role. Here the brain decodes the sounds and structure of language, transforming them into meaningful words and sentences. It's like an orchestra of neurons working together to decode the sounds and meaning hidden within each word. As we communicate, the Broca (also called the convolution of Broca) area of our brain, which is also located in the frontal cortex and filled with neurons involved in speech function, is doing a dance of its own. This region is responsible for organizing and coordinating the motor movements required for speech. Like a skilled conductor, it orchestrates the movements of our lips, tongue, and vocal cords, turning thoughts into articulation. As we listen, our comprehension center in our brain's Wernicke area comes alive, skillfully extracting meaning from the words that greet our ears and eyes.

As we engage in conversation, read captivating stories, or even interpret a simple gesture, a wondrous symphony of neural activity takes place within our minds. My brief and simple explanation shows the marvel of language and communication, which is something that most of us simply take for granted. But for those with language-based learning disorders, it doesn't happen so easily.

### Expressive Language Disorder

People with expressive language disorder have difficulties articulating thoughts and ideas, almost as if a musician was struggling to find the right notes in a lyrical melody. Children with receptive language issues have trouble grasping and understanding the spoken or written word; they comprehend speech but cannot express their understanding. In other words, they hear the words but can't make sense of their meaning. As a result, their speech is halting and dysfluent; they often pepper their speech with "ums" to buy themselves time and figure out how to express themselves. Their first response to a question is usually, "I don't know," another delaying tactic, while their brain scrambles to make sense of the question and come up with a coherent answer. Even when they do respond, they often confuse the order of words or leave out key words such as "on" and "but." They may introduce an unrelated idea into the conversation and have difficulty providing context for their ideas. One patient, Sarah, a self-aware high schooler with a language disorder, exclaimed, "Living with me is like playing a game of Pictionary." What she meant was that she often resorted to miming what she wanted to express due to her struggle to find the correct words. People with LD often jumble the order of sentences and use poor syntax and grammar. Sarah went so far as to often create her own language. She would say "cha" for "yes" and mispronounce or confuse words such as "cannibalism" for "cannabis." Though these malapropisms may seem humorous, and often are, they lead to being misunderstood by peers and adults. The subsequent frustration and embarrassment are real and extremely uncomfortable.

Children with language-based learning disorders encounter significant challenges with everyday communication; it can be a real uphill battle. It's as if the words they want to say are right there, just on the tip of their tongue, but frustratingly inaccessible. This phenomenon originates from the French phrase, "*avoir le mot sur le bout de la langue*," which literally means "having the word on the tip of the tongue." It's a universal experience, observed across diverse languages and cultures. As anyone would, such individuals grow increasingly frustrated by their inability to communicate their thoughts and ideas effectively. This frustration can chip away at their self-esteem, leaving them feeling alienated, even questioning their intelligence. This undeserved sense of inadequacy can lead to a downward spiral, further impacting their academic performance and social interactions. The risk of academic and social failure can loom large due to these language deficits. It's disheartening to witness these bright minds face such obstacles. By acknowledging and understanding the difficulties these children face, we can help them with interventions that work to elevate their confidence and foster a positive trajectory in both their academic and social endeavors.

### Receptive Language Disorders

Receptive language disorders are one of the most debilitating deficits, as children lack the ability to comprehend language. This is not a problem with their ears but is related to how their brain processes language. Children with receptive language disorders experience language as confusing, a blur of words that simply doesn't make sense. Think about how you feel when you hear a foreign language; it appears as a cacophony in which you may be able to isolate and identify a few words but have little understanding. This is the handicap that students with receptive language disorder endure but in their native tongue! As you can imagine, it is very difficult to make friends if you don't understand what your new friend is saying. School becomes another place of frustration and confusion, where you can't meet a teacher's expectations when you simply don't understand the directions. The emotional toll of these challenges is intense. Children feel left out, isolated from both peers and family members, and end up experiencing tremendous failure and frustration.

## Auditory Processing Disorder (APD)

Auditory processing disorder is defined as difficulties in the processing of auditory information in the central nervous system. Here, sufferers have difficulty literally making sense of the auditory information that is presented to them. This is not the same as receptive language disorder; children with receptive language disorder suffer from global deficits in language, whereas children with auditory processing disorder have subtle, nuanced areas of challenge, with typically well-developed receptive and expressive language skills. For example, they may have trouble understanding rapid speech or accented speech but no difficulty following slow, clearly enunciated speech. In addition, they will get easily distracted in noisy environments and can't follow conversation at a party but do perfectly well in a one-on-one situation. All of this makes it extremely difficult to understand, identify, or diagnose. In contrast, children with receptive language disorders always demonstrate these deficits in every situation.

Even though APD is called "auditory" there's nothing wrong with the ears of children suffering from auditory processing deficits. In fact, all of the inner ear structures necessary for hearing are intact. Children with APD have a neurological defect in the pathways from the auditory nerve through the higher auditory pathways in the brain. These pathway disruptions lead to all sorts of problems for children. These challenges show up in the classroom, at home, and on the playground.[3] Children with APD are often highly reactive to noise and prefer to avoid noisy situations such as parties, trains, and stores. Unfortunately, these avoidant behaviors are often mislabeled as anxiety, resulting in the students being treated for anxiety instead of the true cause of their avoidant behaviors. For example, a middle schooler was referred to me due to "phobic" behaviors around trains, stores, and parties. Testing revealed that the origin of these behaviors was auditory processing deficits, leading to effective intervention.

People with APD are very sensitive to noises such as people eating, chewing gum, and drinking, a sensitivity that can be misunderstood as rudeness or even arrogance. Additionally, APD can coexist with other developmental conditions and learning disabilities, such as ADD and autism. It's obviously essential to identify this disorder and treat it effectively. Let's consider a case example.

Charlotte, a vivacious six-year-old girl with sparkling blue eyes, presented as a behavioral enigma to her parents and teachers. Although clearly bright and a precocious reader, Charlotte preferred to spend the majority of her time in the classroom sitting in the book corner, shielding herself with soft pillows and refusing to participate in classroom activities. Her parents commented that at home she was an engaging girl who, although shy and reserved with peers, played nicely with her younger sister and was very cooperative with her parents. Neuropsychological assessment revealed a significant auditory processing disorder. She was overwhelmed by the noise, thus she preferred to avoid the tasks and sit quietly in a corner. In addition, she did not understand the directions for activities because she was distracted by the hubbub in the classroom and thus could not comply with tasks and routines.

As we can see from all these examples, understanding why your child or student behaves the way that he or she does is a crucial first step to addressing the problem. This book is devoted to unpacking not only the "why" our children have trouble, but also the "how" to help them. In the next chapter, we cover nonverbal learning disorder and autism spectrum disorder.

## CHAPTER TWO

# NONVERBAL LEARNING DISORDER AND AUTISM SPECTRUM DISORDER

Imagine children with nonverbal learning disabilities (NVLD) as talented performers on the stage of language, reciting lines and captivating their audience with their eloquence. They excel in verbal communication, but they grapple to make sense of spatial arrangements, which significantly and negatively impacts their ability to perceive the world accurately. They often have a precocious vocabulary and delight their teachers, parents, and peers with an ability to express profound ideas and yet struggle with seemingly routine and mundane tasks such as brushing their teeth, packing their backpacks, and remembering to submit their homework assignments.

These challenges seem enigmatic: "Why can you read and discuss Harry Potter, but you can't tie your shoelaces?" However, there is a common cause: poor visual processing skills. Visual processing is the ability to perceive visual information accurately and efficiently. Children with visual processing difficulties may demonstrate impaired depth perception, misperception or rotation of numbers and letters, and poor visual motor skills, such as those required when catching a ball. In addition, these students often cannot copy letters or adequately perform pencil-and-paper tasks. Organizing papers, managing time, and keeping one's belongings orderly all present significant challenges. These skills are all encoded in the right part of the brain, which deals with numbers and visual information such as maps, graphs, and pictures. The left side of the brain, which is responsible for language, is well developed but the right side of the brain developed erratically in these children.

How do these visual deficits impact academic and social/emotional functioning? Of course, it's nearly impossible to form letters when you can't visualize them properly. Children with NVLD often have illegible handwriting. Writing notes is a challenge, because they have trouble organizing the material on the page and cannot read their own handwriting. Because they have trouble figuring out how to position their fingers, their pencil grip is often incorrect and thus they fatigue easily when writing by hand. Taking tests, even with the benefit of using a Scantron form (a sheet in which students fill in bubbles next to a number representing the answer to a multiple-choice question), is a major struggle: they often fill in the bubbles incorrectly, inadvertently skip a line, and their eyes fatigue from the visual demands.

In addition to these challenges in school, children with NVLD are often clumsy and awkward because they do not perceive space correctly. They tend to be exceedingly unathletic. Reminiscent of the stereotypical bookworm who can't catch a ball, these kids are the awkward, nerdy students who are simply too physically inept to participate in sports. Think of Peter Parker before he transformed into Spider-Man: bookish, bespectacled, awkward, and uncoordinated. Additionally, their lack of athletic prowess is yet another nail in their social coffin as they became known as the kid whom others don't want on their team. Many of my patients with NVLD poignantly describe being bullied and ostracized on the playground solely because they were unable to master basic sport skills. Separately, because they cannot gauge space accurately, these students can be accused of encroaching on other people's physical space. These are the kids who are always stumbling over their own feet, bumping into other children, and inadvertently hurting people.

Stacey, a charming and self-aware teenager with severe dyslexia, exclaimed that she is always dropping things and is so clumsy. When she was younger, she cried when she spilled something because it was such a frustrating experience for her to be unable to control her body or accurately gauge where to place an object. As social human beings, we always want to avoid situations where we could potentially be embarrassed or rejected, so these kinds of mishaps understandably lead to intense social anxiety and avoidance of social situations.

As these children develop academically, they may compensate for their visual-spatial issues in reading and writing with their strong language skills. Still, they continue to struggle in math and science because these subjects are more dependent on visual information. In addition, because their visual memory—that is, recall for visual items such as numbers and designs—is often compromised, they have great difficulty retaining numerical facts. It's hard to imagine, but for people with NVLD, simply processing visual information is laborious and they work slowly due to impaired visual efficiency.

Writing can also be a struggle due to their difficulty in organizing and sequencing, which is the skill set for ordering and organizing objects, ideas, or sentences in a logical and consistent manner. It extends to performing tasks such as cleaning your room or cooking from a recipe. We all need to be able to follow directions, organize our materials, and understand where objects belong. Similarly, with writing, we need to create a logical flow of ideas and construct sentences that convey progression and logic sequence from topic sentence to supporting sentences to conclusions. Although children with NVLD often have wonderful ideas, their writing can be disorganized and tangential. Understandably, reading speed can also be compromised by poor visual processing, which makes the pleasure of reading turn into a frustrating and demanding task. So it's understandable that these students have difficulty complying with tasks that require visual sequencing, including tasks such as standing in an orderly line with other classmates or finding the correct page in a book. These are things that many people take for granted. People with NVLD struggle profoundly with everyday tasks, which takes a tremendous toll on their self-esteem and leads to feelings of immense incompetence.

Sue Thompson was one of the first clinicians to correctly identify these students. Her book, *The Source for NVLD*, helpfully lists the characteristics of the nonverbal learning-disabled student who is at risk for academic, social, and emotional failures. It is a classic must-read for all parents and teachers confronted with NVLD. She explains that these children are rigid and have difficulty with transitions. As young children, these are the kids who tantrum upon leaving the park or cry every morning before going to school. The rigidity manifests itself in what can be seen as "stubborn and strong willed." They often hold tight to their ideas and cannot flexibly shift from one topic of conversation to another. Their brain gets stuck almost like a record in a groove and it can be painful to shift. It takes them more time to execute transitions as well.

As they get older, transitions continue to be a problem, and without a parent or caregiver to help, these shifts can take a very long time for them to complete. Think of all the visual steps required to leave the house, for example. First, it's extremely difficult for them to stop what-ever activity with which they are engaged in order to enter a different space. Then they need to get everything collected, organize a backpack, and put on a coat. All of these tasks are performed at what seems to be glacial speed. It can be a truly frustrating process both physically and mentally. Even transitions within the school day, between classrooms or from work to play time, require more time for these children. Children with NVLD simply operate at a different speed than other children. Recognizing that they need more time to prepare mentally and physi-cally can greatly facilitate transitions.

Socially, children with NVLD can be oblivious to hierarchy and body language because they are not taking in the visual input correctly. We can understand this phenomenon with the idea of "garbage in, garbage out," or GIGO, which refers to the idea that in any system, the quality of output is determined by the quality of the input. In other words, these children are not accurately recognizing visual cues such as head nod-ding, eye contact, and body language. Thus, they often completely mis-understand the situation and remain bewildered when, to their peers, it is blindingly obvious.

Emily, a stylish and precocious tween with NVLD, had a tendency to address her teachers as if they were her peers, calling them by their first names and responding to their directions as if they were optional. She tended to get embroiled in arguments and was widely seen as uncoopera-tive. This wasn't intentional. Instead, she was "tone deaf" and simply didn't understand that she was being disrespectful. Similarly, Arielle, a lithe dancer with dark hair, suffered from social isolation despite an extroverted personality. She continually committed social faux pas that sadly alienated her peers. For example, while at a crowded dance party with her friends, Arielle would take her hairbrush out of her bag and begin to brush her long hair right in the middle of the party. The children, knowing that it was inappropriate, scrambled to escape the flying hair strands, and Arielle unwittingly caused a scene that was fodder for drama within her middle school class. In school, she would stretch her body or lift her leg over her head in odd contortions that made her peers uncomfortable. But Arielle had absolutely no clue that her behavior was in any way off-putting. Instead, she simply felt shunned and isolated, wondering why.

Meet Leslie, a dynamic and bright young woman in her mid-twenties who faced the complexities of living with a nonverbal learning disorder. As a graduate student in public history at a prestigious institution, she possessed remarkable comprehension and easily grasped the materials presented in class. However, even though her reading skills were excellent, completing assignments proved to be a struggle. Leslie also faced ongoing challenges with personal hygiene and struggled to keep her room tidy, which led to feelings of shame. Living with a roommate, she was totally oblivious to the physical space they shared. This led to disagreeable confrontations despite her feelings of friendship and the desire to get along with her roommate. Leslie frequently left dishes in the sink, was messy in the bathroom, and ignored cleaning communal areas. At school, Leslie found it difficult to connect with classmates. She carried a deep sense of insecurity, believing that her peers were more academically advanced and "together" compared to herself. All of these hurdles were a direct result of her nonverbal learning disorder.

It's essential to understand that a nonverbal learning disorder affects several different aspects of a person's life. For Leslie, it impacted her academic performance, personal organization, and social interactions. Despite her intellectual capabilities, the disorder created challenges in her daily life and an erosion of her self-confidence.

On a positive note, individuals with NVLD tend to be excellent readers and are highly verbal and articulate. Professions that have an emphasis on reading and writing are well-suited for them, including professors; researchers, especially in the social science realm; editors; and lawyers. However, both disorders—language-based learning and nonverbal learning—often lead to more specific academic disorders in reading, writing, and math. Let's take a look.

## READING DISORDERS

One of the most well-known reading disorders is dyslexia—experienced by Albert Einstein, Thomas Edison, Leonardo da Vinci, George

Washington, and yes, Tom Cruise. Throughout history, numerous individuals from various fields have overcome dyslexia to achieve greatness and leave indelible marks on the world. Individuals with dyslexia tend to see the world in a visual manner and are often quite artistic and creative. Visual-spatial thinkers see patterns and can come up with ideas that are innovative and exciting. Thus, artists, designers, inventors, and architects are some of the professions that benefit from those with strong visual-spatial thinking.

Broadly defined, dyslexia refers to difficulty reading, but in no way does it define the potential or capabilities of those who have it. From brilliant scientists, influential politicians, and business leaders to iconic entertainers and creatives, many have shown us that dyslexia is no barrier to success and accomplishment.

Children with dyslexia demonstrate poor reading fluency, impaired reading accuracy, and deficient reading comprehension. They have a hard time reading smoothly and accurately. Understanding what they read can be very tricky. They typically present early, around six or seven, when their peers are learning how to read. Students reverse letters and experience something called impoverished sight vocabulary, with a limited number of written words they recognize automatically. They have dysfluency, which is a choppy reading style wherein they stumble over words. Importantly, they can miss the entire meaning of sentences, because they can't recognize key words in a paragraph. Early on, you might notice that your student mixes up letters, has trouble recognizing common words, and that his or her reading lacks "flow." These challenges may partially arise from a visual processing impairment as discussed earlier in the chapter, wherein they see the letters jumbled or floating around in a confused order. This peculiar presentation is then compounded by language-based deficits, along with a weak working memory.[1]

Working memory involves the mental manipulation of information. More specifically, it's the ability to hold information in mind and use it to execute cognitive tasks. Working memory is what holds new information in place so the brain can work with it briefly and connect it with other information. Think of working memory as a sticky note in our brain where we hold and play with information. It's basically our ability to remember layers of information and use that information simultaneously while doing different tasks in our minds. Having a strong working memory is incredibly useful in everyday life. It helps us remember a phone number long enough to dial it or understand and remember a story while we read it. It's like our brain's multitasking ability, allowing us to keep important bits of information in mind while focusing on the task at hand. Some of us have large mental sticky notes and can hold a lot of information, whereas others find it really challenging to keep many things in mind at once. Children with neurocognitive challenges often present with poor working memory, since acquiring academic skills is dependent on information processing. Importantly, because reading depends on the ability to recognize words to build up a sight vocabulary and make connections, a poor working memory interferes with acquiring these skills.

Sarah, a sensitive, empathetic seven-year-old girl who loved to look at books, offers a good illustration of dyslexia. Sarah seemed to enjoy reading books, but her phonics skill, which is the ability to match sound with symbol in letter identification, was exceptionally low and her sight word vocabulary was very poor. She seemed to know the storyline and characters in a book but over time her mother realized that Sarah was actually doing something that many children with dyslexia do to compensate: she was memorizing the books in school as they were read to her! This is quite an accomplishment in itself. Imagine Sarah's ability: her "reading" was actually pure memorization! One could say that she was in fact quite capable and brilliant, which is exactly the case for many students with dyslexia. Unsurprisingly, a neuropsychological evaluation revealed that Sarah had severe dyslexia. She was referred for Orton-Gillingham instruction, a specialized, data-based remediation geared to improve her phonics skills. As a result, her reading improved, although she continues to present, at age ten, with choppy, dysfluent, and slow reading skills.

## WRITTEN EXPRESSION DISORDER

Compromised written expression is another byproduct of language-based learning disorders. Since writing is an academic skill that primarily depends on a facility with words, it's easy to see how important the skill of written expression is to education and to one's world at large. If we can't express ourselves verbally in a coherent and organized manner, we won't be able to write in a logical fashion. Our vocabulary will be impoverished, and we'll tend to write in simple, short sentences that lack richness and nuance. Critically, other people will be unable to understand or follow. Written expression disorder also encompasses difficulties with organizing and writing thoughts; using proper grammar, punctuation, and syntax; coming up with evocative words; supporting ideas with sufficient detail; and generally conveying ideas coherently on paper. Imagine writing an essay or simple paragraph for a school assignment. For most of us, the task is relatively straightforward, not requiring tremendous effort. We can easily put our ideas into words, structure sentences properly, and make sure our writing flows smoothly. If not Shakespearean, we are certainly able to be understood. For students with written expression disorder, the process becomes a Herculean task.

A person with this impairment is akin to an inexperienced builder. They might have excellent ideas, just like anyone else, but when it comes to translating those ideas—erecting the actual edifice—they struggle. They have the materials but lack the blueprints. Furthermore, as laborers, these builders have shaky hands while working with tools; students with written expression disorder have graphomotor difficulties, rendering their handwriting sloppy and laborious. Their poor penmanship comes from visual processing deficits, as we discussed earlier, wherein letters can be seen as jumbled and in the wrong order; individuals are also unable to form letters correctly. Furthermore, the muscle tone of these students often is low; they have trouble gripping the pencil correctly and fatigue easily to the point that they often complain that their hands hurt after writing. In the classroom, these learners are at a disadvantage as they may have difficulty following directions, participating in class, retaining information, taking notes, and producing content in class, on homework, and on tests. It's essential to recognize that these students are not lazy or unintelligent. Notably, these difficulties with written expression, along with trouble following classroom rules and expectations, commonly co-occur with the learning disorders mentioned earlier, such as nonverbal and other language-based learning disorders.

## MATH DISORDERS

Dyscalculia is a deficit in the ability to perform math-related tasks, a process that can become overwhelming and frustrating. Children who suffer have difficulty understanding or recalling basic mathematical concepts such as number recognition, counting, or understanding mathematical symbols and operation. Imagine how incredibly hard math would be without these foundational concepts intact. It's important to recognize that learning disabilities often have complex and interconnected roots, with individuals experiencing challenges in multiple areas of learning. Dyscalculia can stem from and coexist with different learning disorders and developmental conditions. Although it's primarily associated with difficulties in understanding and processing numerical information, the disorder is linked to various others, such as dyslexia, attention deficit hyperactivity disorder, working memory, and executive functioning deficits, as well as visual-spatial processing issues. Children with language-based disorders in particular may have difficulty with word problems. They can experience challenges with not only numbers but numeric symbols, such as those for division and multiplication, and other mathematical text. Compromised working memory skills significantly impact a student's ability to do math, as he or she has difficulty retaining numerical facts and math rules for procedural accuracy. Also, poor abstract reasoning skills lead to difficulty setting up problems and applying algorithms, all important parts of the processes required for successful completion. Math often requires understanding shapes, spatial relationships, and patterns, with which children with NVLD are typically weaker due to their visual-spatial processing deficits.

In addition to the academic toll that nonverbal learning deficits exact, there is an equally profound social and emotional one that comes while living with these challenges. Children can suffer tremendously because they are not as competent as their peers. They are constantly comparing themselves unfavorably to others and begin to internalize a sense of themselves as ineffectual. Children often verbalize, "I am bad at math," "I hate reading," "I cannot understand the teacher," and "I won't do this work; it's boring!" They understandably avoid academics but also end up trying to circumvent social situations. Because they feel terrible about themselves, they'll do anything to avoid the kind of comparisons that they inevitably make when they get together with their peers. This is not only heartbreaking, but totally corrosive to their self-esteem. Children without learning issues can often be found comparing test grades, talking about their schoolwork, and sharing their classroom experiences. The neurodivergent child cannot contribute to these conversations, so he or she ends up feeling painfully left out. You're likely reading this book because you know about this and have seen it happen with your own child or student. You've watched them developmentally shy away from growth-producing social situations, limiting their exposure and opportunity to practice social skills and hold their own with group banter. But it doesn't have to be this way.

## AUTISM SPECTRUM DISORDER (ASD)

Let's move on to autism spectrum disorder (ASD), a neurodevelopmental disorder that affects how individuals perceive the world, communicate, and interact with others. ASD has been in the news quite a bit these last few years with evidence that it has become more common in recent decades.[2] ASD is characterized by deficits in multiple areas of development including social relations and communication, impacting nearly every aspect of life and across a range of interests and activities. From difficulty socializing with peers and communicating appropriately to simply understanding their own or other people's feelings, people with autism are markedly ill-attuned to social dynamics. They are often preoccupied with a rigid range of interests, engaging in restrictive, repetitive, and stereotypical behaviors. Some say that Einstein, Isaac Newton, and Michelangelo all exhibited behaviors indicative of ASD from difficulties with social interactions to eccentric behaviors. Newton was known for being socially withdrawn and introverted, spending long hours immersed in his studies and research; he spent his time constructing intricate models and conducting experiments to test his theories, working alone and rarely engaging in personal or social interactions.

People with ASD can become quite agitated when their routines are disrupted or when faced with overstimulation. Although their academic difficulties are more variable, they can also have poor working memory along with impaired selective attention and complex information processing. ASD is a condition that affects how the brain develops and functions. Although the exact cause is not fully understood, researchers have found that certain areas of the brain may be structurally different in people with autism. The most likely neurobiological basis for autism involves abnormalities across a network of subcortical and cortical structures.[3] In the brain, there are three different regions responsible for various tasks. Some areas, called subcortical structures, help with the processing of information and sending messages between different parts of the brain. Among those with autism, these areas might not work as expected, leading to differences in how people with autism perceive and respond to their surroundings. Other brain regions called the cortex are involved in complex thinking, understanding emotions, and processing sensory information. For those with autism, certain parts of the cortex might show differences in how they are connected or structured, which can impact their social interactions and communication skills. Mirror neurons in the brain help us understand and imitate others' actions and feelings. In people with autism, this system appears to be inefficient, making it challenging to interpret others' emotions and social cues. Genetics can also play a role.

Individuals with ASD often develop significant expertise in one area, for example, science, transportation, or baseball facts, and can appear as a savant within this area. This expertise reflects their capacity for hyper-focused attention and their ability to remember large amounts of factual information. However, they may then present with deficits in areas in which they lack basic skills or do not have interest. Temple Grandin is a wonderful example of someone with ASD. An animal behavior expert and advocate for people with autism, she's written extensively about her experiences. Her life and accomplishments were the subject of a wonderful HBO biographical film. She has used her unique perspective and thought patterns to explain animal behavior, as she "thinks in pictures" and experiences sensory stimuli much the way animals do. For example, she designed a humane chute to bring cows to slaughter in a way that calms the animals. Her thought patterns are representative of people with ASD, as she is hyper-aware, noticing details that people with more typical brains do not.

A hallmark of ASD is tremendous difficulty socializing. Children with ASD are the ones who stand out on the playground, at parties, and in school, as they cannot easily engage with peers. They may use "stereotype" language, which is communication restricted to one-word utterances or stringing together unrelated facts. They often don't look directly at others, preferring to gaze downward, and can often appear entirely uninterested in conversation or connection. Some people with autism tend to repeat words or sentences, referred to as "echolalia" and "scripting." They may quote extensively from movies or TV shows or repeat the same ideas in a conversation. Rigidity and repetition define people with ASD; think of a record player that repetitively goes over the same groove. People with ASD cannot stop their repetitive behavior, such as twirling their hair, flapping their hands, and playing with objects. These behaviors are called "stimming," as they stimulate the brain and initiate a cycle of repetition that soothes them.

My patient, Eliza, an articulate and insightful college student with ASD who is a talented writer and passionate advocate for climate change, is very aware of her challenges. She plans for and incorporates "stimming" times, when she obsessively strokes her cat's fur for several hours. Eliza explained to me that this activity is calming to her and when she doesn't make time for it, she feels highly distressed.

Overactivity to stimuli poses yet another challenge for people suffering from this disorder. Their perception of noise, light, smell, and taste are very different from the neurotypical individual. They may react with pain to seemingly innocuous noises, such as somebody eating, or may get completely overwhelmed by loud, crowded environments. It's important to remember that children with ASD are not trying to be rude, controlling, or bossy when they request quiet or dim lights. Sadly, however, they are often misinterpreted in such ways.

Eliza, who lives with her parents, has negotiated this terrain by setting up a schedule for when they use certain rooms in order to control the noise level and sensory input in her house. At the same time, fascinatingly, people with ASD often do not seem to feel pain or fear when you would expect them to. They might run into a wall or bang their head repeatedly because they simply do not feel the pain associated with these behaviors. There are varied hypotheses for the decreased pain sensitivity demonstrated by some people with ASD. Certain repetitive behaviors such as rocking and flapping produce endorphins and may dull pain. A number of researchers have suggested that excessive brain opioid activity is not only the etiology of low pain sensitivity but underlies many of the symptoms of ASD, including motor hyperactivity, repetitive behaviors, and reduced socialization.[4]

As an example, let's take a look at the fictional character Raymond, played by Dustin Hoffman in the movie *Rain Man*. Raymond perfectly represents several of these characteristics. He watches his favorite TV show, *The People's Court*, and often repeats the show's host's name, Judge Wapner, as a way to cope with stress and anxiety. His line, "Four minutes to Wapner," has become part of the cultural lexicon! Raymond also struggles with nonverbal communicative behaviors. He rarely maintains eye contact and demonstrates a preoccupation with numbers and routines. He adheres to strict daily rituals and becomes really upset when they're disrupted. He's also highly sensitive to loud noises and bright lights, which cause him distress. However, Raymond is also the character in the movie who has superb recall and can compute extraordinarily complex calculations. He is both brilliant and limited at the same time, reflective of many people with ASD who harbor extraordinary mental capacities in some realms and significantly deficient social/interpersonal skills.

People with autism also can find it challenging to understand social cues and emotions. They are often confused and bewildered by the emotional responses of others. Sometimes, they can locate a specific feeling, such as sadness, anger, and happiness, in a very narrow manner. For example, they might say, "Oh, you are sad because you are crying," but completely miss the reason behind the sadness, even when it is a completely obvious loss or failure. They simply can't process feelings the way neurotypical people do. This can be very frustrating for family members, peers, and teachers. The good news is that parents and teachers can educate people with ASD about their feelings and help them understand social situations. Breaking down the situation and explaining very concretely what is going on both emotionally and interpersonally is extremely helpful. For example, when you watch a TV show with your child, you can talk about cause and effect: "The father is angry with his son because the son lied about doing his homework." What we all need to understand is how people with ASD process information, which is one tree at a time, to help them understand the complexity of the forest. In other words, they miss the forest for the trees. They can describe each tree in wondrous depth, focus with exquisite sensitivity to each leaf and how the tree communicates with its neighbors, but miss the wider perspective of the forest.

Alex, for example, is a brilliant, soft-spoken tween who possessed an encyclopedic knowledge of weather. When talking about his trip to Washington State, he explained each day's weather in vivid detail, including degrees of temperature, percentage of rain, and chance of any weather events. Yet completely absent from his report was any other aspect of the trip, including what he saw or even with whom he went. People with ASD have an inexhaustible fund of knowledge in specific areas, acting almost like human computers in their ability to focus with a laser intensity on a topic. This hyper-focus can be a superpower and enables them to do amazing cognitive feats. In fact, autistic individuals once were labeled "idiot savants" in recognition of their talents, such as rapid calculation of numerical facts, and their drawbacks, such as their inability to negotiate social situations. *Savant* comes from the Latin word *sapere* ("to be wise") and shares roots with the English words *sapient* ("possessing great wisdom") and *sage* ("very wise").[5]

Other strengths of people with ASD include an incredible attunement to details that enables them to perform obsessive, detail-oriented work that other people would see as boring and tedious. In addition, they can solve complicated problems as visual-spatial learners and often make excellent computer programmers and technicians. It's important to recognize that ASD is not a disease or a result of poor parenting. It is a lifelong condition among individuals who have unique and powerful strengths and abilities.

A delightful patient of mine, Matt, is a bespectacled, geeky twelve-year-old boy who came to me when he was an eighth grader in a competitive private school. Despite holding his own academically, he presented with significant social difficulties. One of the first things I noticed was the way he spoke in a flat, dull, monotone voice and his inability to maintain eye contact with me. Matt regaled me with his knowledge. He was obsessed with transportation and had an encyclopedic retention of any facts related to trains, planes, and cars, which he recited ad nauseum, in detail. In conversation with me, he had no awareness whatsoever of how boring it was for me, the listener, to hear someone recounting train schedules in excruciating detail! When I was able to divert him from that topic by explaining gently to him that this would be considered boring and that he has other interests and experiences that I would love to hear about, he was able to express interest in me and converse nicely. His obsessive focus on his own interests stemmed from his brain's hard-wiring and his difficulty noticing his impact on other people. When I cued him, he was then able to shift topics, because he genuinely wanted to connect with me. However, in school, he didn't have anyone to help him and therefore was shunned by his peers, a constant source of iso-lation, which he poignantly articulated when he announced, "I have no friends."

If we can understand the hardwiring of our children's brains, it will help us recognize what is going on with them in every arena: at home, with peers, and in school. Our children struggle with everyday tasks and meeting expectations because their skills are not up to these challenges. This also takes a heavy emotional toll on them, as they feel like such failures. So our job with our neurodivergent children is both to help them improve their academic and social skills and to help them grow into confident and competent adults. Now that we better understand the *why* of these academic and social/emotional challenges, let's dig into how we can help our children both emotionally and academically.

CHAPTER THREE

# THE ABCs OF TESTING

I'm proud of you. You've decided to have your child tested. Good for you, and most importantly, good for your child. Here are the basics or what I call testing ABCs.

Evaluations are great because they are an essential component of understanding what is going on with your child's school performance, social skills, and mental well-being. Once you find out what is contributing to your child's challenges, you are in a much better position to help him or her, because understanding the root cause of almost anything is the absolute best way to figure out a solution. In my practice, I begin with a comprehensive neuropsychological evaluation, which encompasses several key parts:

- learning style
- academic skills
- memory
- attention
- motor skills
- social/emotional functioning
- reasoning
- problem solving

But first, let's take a look at the history of testing. What we know of as modern IQ testing began with Alfred Binet, a Frenchman who developed a test (appropriately called the Binet test) to identify students with learning difficulties and provide improved education services. Binet's test rapidly became popular in the United States. It had a wide application for diverse purposes, including use by the army and the police to screen applicants. It was used in schools to determine eligibility for special programs—either remedial or enriched—and, unfortunately, to provide fodder to a now discredited theory of eugenics. The dark side of IQ testing is that it also was used to argue for the inherent superiority of one race over another, in which, for example, forcible sterilizations were carried out on "feeble-minded" individuals. Of course, gratefully, these tremendously abusive practices have stopped, and IQ testing is now widely used, particularly in schools, to assess children and recommend intervention and accommodations.

## WHAT IS AN IQ TEST?

Simply put, an IQ test is designed to reveal a child's potential and give us an idea of his or her learning style. Is he a visual learner? Auditory learner? Does she have an amazing memory, or is she extremely slow at some tasks? The IQ test can be viewed as a preliminary blueprint to identify patterns and begin to figure out what is really going on with your child.

The IQ test is divided into four indices: verbal, visual spatial, working memory, and processing speed—subjects on which your child's performance is compared across indices as well as subtests to create a cognitive profile. For example, although children may be highly verbal, they can lose points for speed on the visual-spatial index. They may do really well with the blocks and puzzles but bomb the memory section. What is extremely important to note is that the actual numbers are insignificant. Instead, it's the patterns that are the most revealing and helpful, giving neurocognitive testers valuable information regarding your child's learning profile. You see, the numbers are simply an average of the subtests, and your child's performance will most likely vary on each subtest. This is the nature of neurocognitive differences, where children's abilities are typically all over the map. As experts, we essentially ignore the numbers and focus instead on the patterns. A skilled tester will walk you through these patterns, helping you see what they reveal so that you can fully understand what the test data means.

Through testing, you'll also gain an understanding of your child's academic skills; in other words, how he or she performs basic tasks such as reading, writing, and math. All recorded scores are normed, meaning your child is compared with other children of the same age so that you can get a sense of how behind or advanced they are. In a sense, you can view the IQ as "potential," whereas the academic tests reveal what is really happening now, in the classroom. Academic tests are typically comprehensive, meaning they offer a good picture of different types of reading and math skills as well as handwriting and spelling capabilities. With that important information gleaned from testing, practitioners can compare a child's potential with his or her reality, which is where the good stuff comes in: understanding what challenges your child is facing in the context of their performance. In this way, we can begin to figure out why they are under- or overperforming.

Once I understand a child's basic learning style and skills, it is time for me to delve into the more nuanced and exciting neuropsychological functions, such as speech, language, attention, memory, and motor skills. I typically administer a plethora of different normed assessments designed to evaluate your child's proficiency in each area. These tests are invaluable to understanding exactly what is going on and, importantly, which specific interventions will best help your child. Critically, as these tests pinpoint the specific nature of each disorder, they set the stage for the recommendations for accommodations and modifications that your child can receive in school to jump-start their success.

A typical neuropsychological battery covers several neurocognitive domains, including general intelligence, academic achievement, speech and language, attention, memory, auditory processing, visuo-spatial processing, and motor skills. A personality section is often included to provide insight into any relevant emotional issues, including self-esteem, anxiety, depression, and other aspects of social/emotional functioning. The report carefully details the nuances of the patient's challenges and strengths. Personally, I am dedicated to authentically knowing my patients, as the best results and best testing practices include a detailed background section that encompasses development, family history, behavioral observations, social/emotional/academic functioning, and medical history.

## CHOOSING THE TESTS

Selecting a test battery is specific to the patient; however, there is a core battery of tests that provides basic information on overall cognitive functioning. The evaluator can then add further tests tailored to the individual student. I find that many patients understand the test results better when they have an initial understanding of the makeup of the tests. Some of the most frequently used tests include the following.

The Wechsler IQ tests (WISC) are widely used as a baseline of performance, a screening of potential challenges, and an overall measure of academic potential. David Wechsler, a psychologist, developed this test to assess intelligence in a practical and clinical way. He posited that intelligence was made up of several domains such as verbal skills, visual-spatial abilities, working memory, and processing speed. Therefore, the WISC scores for all of these, in contrast to the Binet, the original IQ test, which consisted of a single score.[1] Let's take a look at some of the different indices.

The verbal portion of the WISC evaluates vocabulary by asking students to define words. The WISC also looks at how your child uses language to categorize items. For example, I might ask, "How are a table and a chair alike?" The answer I'm looking for—that they are both furniture—would reflect the knowledge of a category. Finally, the WISC test looks at how your child uses language to describe and analyze social situations. For example, I might ask, "What would you do if you found someone else's wallet in a store?" As you can see, the language portion of the WISC reveals your child's verbal abilities. After testing, I can confidently predict how well a student will do in school based on these responses and their associated scores. In many ways, I (and all testers) have to be great multitaskers, because while conducting the testing and asking these revealing questions, we also watch a student's behavior during the testing. We ask ourselves: Are they restless or fidgety? Do they often say "I don't know"? Are they easily distracted, or do they stray off topic? Do they get frustrated or say that they're stupid? Can they express themselves in an articulate and concise manner? All these observations—both large and small—round out the picture and help us understand your child's learning style.

The visual-spatial portion of the WISC looks at how adept your child is at analyzing geometric designs, recognizing patterns using pictures and blocks, and using their reasoning skills with designs and puzzles. Tests are also timed, so it is an opportunity for the evaluator to assess your child's speed and efficiency with visual material. We really get quite a good idea of how comfortable a student is with visual material such as graphs, math, and maps. We look carefully at how they approach problems: Are they methodical and thoughtful? Do they have a strategy, or do they just haphazardly arrange the materials? Do they get easily frustrated and give up? Do they persist beyond the time limits? Personally, I invest a lot of time with careful observation of the whole child in a holistic assessment.

The working memory index of the WISC evaluates your child's ability to process and retain numbers and pictures. This gives us a good idea of his or her ability to process auditory and visual information. When testers talk about "working memory," the reference to memory is a little bit of a misnomer, because it's not assessing long-term recall, but rather one's ability to receive information, keep it in mind, and then have the ability to express it. This is a valuable school-related skill that impacts a student's ability to follow directions, keep on track with a task, and transfer information from one format to another, such as translating graphs and understanding cartoons.

Processing speed, another index, consists of two timed tasks: one asks your child to copy symbols using a key and the second asks your child to indicate similar symbols on a line. With this assessment, I can get a very good idea of a student's pencil-and-paper skills, especially his or her speed of copying but also accuracy and legibility. I can also understand how quickly and accurately he or she processes visual information such as letters and numbers.

Although the WISC measures cognitive function, it is not intended to assess academic performance. Instead, a wide variety of academic skills-based tests are frequently used. The Wechsler Individual Achievement Test, fourth edition (WIAT-4), is coordinated with the Wechsler IQ tests to provide the evaluator with a standardized achievement score that is statistically comparable with the IQ scores.[2] This is important, because when a tester sees a large discrepancy between intellectual ability and academic performance, it often means there's a learning disorder. The WIAT assesses a wide range of academic skills, including reading accuracy, reading comprehension, numerical facility, spelling, and written expression. However, the WIAT's assessment of academic skills can be superficial, in that it asks students to read several lines instead of full paragraphs. Instead, there are other academic tests, such as the Gray Oral Reading Test, fifth edition,[3] which are more detailed or focused, giving testers a further nuanced appreciation of a child's reading and writing skills.

The GORT-5 evaluates reading accuracy, fluency, and comprehension with multisentence paragraphs. The test of written language scores a student's writing on diverse criteria, including the organization of the paragraph; that is, does the paragraph open with a topic sentence? Are there supporting and concluding sentences? Is there flow from one paragraph to the other? The test reveals theme development: Does the writer develop the theme throughout the essay? Are the ideas well supported? Does the writer introduce tangential information? These tests truly reveal how your child performs in school, as the tasks very closely approximate academic expectations in reading and writing.[4]

There is also a plethora of speech and language tests ranging from quick and superficial assessments of receptive and expressive language, such as the Peabody Picture Vocabulary Test, which assesses a student's ability to either name pictures (expressive) or indicate understanding of a word by pointing to one of four pictures that best describes the word (receptive).[5] In this test, for example, the word "sitting" is displayed with four pictures. A student is then asked to point to the picture that depicts a child who is sitting in a chair.

The Clinical Evaluation of Language Fundamentals, fifth edition, is more nuanced and comprehensive. It's widely used to effectively assess diverse speech and language skills, such as sentence structure, syntax, grammar, auditory memory, and word definition skills.[6]

Memory provides another domain of assessment. Memory is a complicated construct that requires careful assessment with varied memory tests, such as the Wide Range Assessment of Memory and Learning, third edition.[7] Using it, a child is asked to recall a list of words and a story to evaluate auditory memory. Children are also asked to copy designs from recall to evaluate visual memory. Last, children are shown, and asked to commit to memory, pictures of several scenes including a beach scene and a grocery store. Then they are presented with a similar picture with some missing or changed details. For example, in the first picture, a boy plays with a blue pail. In the second picture, the color of the pail is changed to red. The student is then asked to circle the missing or changed details of the scene. This test excellently measures visual attention to details and visual recall.

As evaluators, we need to understand how your child processes visual and auditory information to gain a clear picture of his or her learning style. We can also understand how comfortable your child is with keeping information in mind and then accurately demonstrating that information, a key skill in school. We often give multistep directions and present students with information that they need to retain and absorb. Thus, we use these tasks to see how adept children are at following directions and absorbing both visual and auditory information. At the same time, we are evaluating their ability to use information effectively.

Attention is an essential skill to assess, as it contributes significantly to academic success. When we think of attention, we think of paying attention to something or someone. But in the realm of neurocognitive psychology, attention is really the ability to maintain focus on a particular task. It encompasses a range of neurocognitive skills, such as impulse control, resistance to distraction, and the ability to execute transitions. Cognitive rigidity is another hallmark of attention problems. Children with ADD, for example, have significant difficulty shifting between tasks and perspectives. Abilities such as these can sometimes be difficult to assess, so revealing them requires multiple assessment measures. The Continuous Performance Test is the gold standard of attention tests.[8] A test of vigilance that requires attention to a visual or auditory presentation of randomly occurring letters, it asks a student to either respond or inhibit a response to the letters. Here a child is presented with random letters and instructed to press the space bar on a computer after each letter except the letter $X$. In this way, we can get a sense of how evenly the child sustains attention as we measure the speed of the response. The test clocks in at fourteen minutes, so we can really see whether a child is able to sustain attention. Of course, it's natural for a student to want to hit the space bar every time a letter appears, so the test also requires a student to inhibit their response when they see the letter $X$. This test is designed to be quite boring and frustrating, as it measures pure ability to attend, the ability to keep focusing even when it is boring, impulse control, and ability to adjust to oddly spaced intervals.

Two other widely used tests include the Stroop Color and Word Test, a measure of selective or focused attention, and the Wisconsin Card Sorting Test, a measure of cognitive flexibility, or the ability to shift tasks efficiently.[9] Here a student is presented with cards that they need to sort according to criteria such as shape, number, and color. The "trick" is that the criteria change after every ten correct responses, so a student needs to be flexible and recognize when the criteria shift. If a student is rigid, he or she continues repeating the same pattern instead of pivoting to a different pattern, demonstrating difficulty with executing transitions in daily life and conversations.

Because teaching is often verbal, auditory processing and auditory attention are crucial skills that can really help your student and greatly contribute to academic performance. We look very closely and carefully at auditory processing, as I have found that it plays an essential role in the classroom. I have evaluated many children with undiagnosed auditory processing challenges. The SCAN-C Test for Auditory Processing Disorders in Children is an excellent screening assessment to determine whether your child has auditory processing or auditory attention challenges.[10] This test provides four scores on subtests, tapping auditory attention and discrimination in both ears. For example, a child undergoing this test listens to competing words piped into both ears. They then are asked to say the word that they heard in the right ear. Students are also asked to discriminate foreground and background noise, another essential skill in the classroom. This test is terrific, as evaluators get a comprehensive profile of these skills, which they use to make important recommendations for success at home and at school.

Facility with pencil-and-paper tasks is a critical component of academic success. Your child needs to write legibly, copy from the board, and fill out worksheets. The Beery Test of Visual Motor Integration can evaluate your child's ability to copy designs, which are presented in varying levels from easy (a circle) to complicated (multidimensional rings). Seeing how a student performs helps us determine graphomotor skills, which simply means the ability to copy designs.

## AUTISM

If I think a patient may fall on the autism spectrum, I utilize a test called the Autism Diagnostic Observation Schedule-2.[11] This test assesses social and communicative behaviors relevant to an autism diagnosis. The Behavior Assessment System for Children[12] is a questionnaire for parents and teachers to complete about a student's attentional, social, somatic, and other behavioral realms. Though it's not specific to autism, it can be helpful to screen for general social/emotional problems, which are common in autism. In addition, the Social Responsiveness Scale, second edition (SRS-2) identifies the presence and severity of social impairment characteristics of individuals within the autism spectrum.[13] These tests create a basic set that can be adjusted for each student by adding or removing tests, based on what they need.

## WHAT ABOUT SOCIAL/EMOTIONAL FUNCTIONING?

Beyond the confines of assessments and test scores lies the vibrant world of childhood, teeming with emotions, imagination, and individuality. Children are not merely students; they are a tapestry of feelings, curiosity, and an innate thirst for connection. Integral to their journey is not just academic growth, but the intricate dance of socialization, friendships, and finding their place within the community. Therefore, as neurocognitive psychologists, we pay a lot of attention to a child's well-being, so we need to have a way to assess what's going on socially and emotionally, truly critical areas. Children are multidimensional, often with complex, emotional responses to their academic and emotional challenges. It is essential for the testing to reveal the impact of what I call the "lived experience" of a disability. In this way we can provide an empathetic perspective. Also, many times, a child experiences social/ emotional challenges separate from the neurocognitive challenge that also needs to be addressed.

To discover what is happening in the emotional interior of a child's life, I typically use personality assessments. You may have heard of the Rorschach test, an inkblot test that has been used for the past one hundred years. First developed by psychologist Herman Rorschach, the general principle behind the Rorschach test is that your child projects or externalizes his or her feelings onto these ambiguous inkblots. I use the Exner, a system that scores your child's responses to the Rorschach using criteria that have been standardized with thousands of children. We can see if children see the blot realistically, how they feel about themselves, their coping styles, and whether they meet criteria for various psychiatric disorders. I don't use the Rorschach as a standalone test, but I find it helpful as a piece of the puzzle when assessing a student's social/emotional functioning. My experience is that the actual content of the responses to the blots can also be very revealing, giving me valuable insight into a child's struggles.

For example, the first card of the Rorschach deck is typically seen as two hooded figures. When I presented it to my patient Ben, an articulate adolescent struggling with attention and learning challenges, he described the image as "an unknown creature from a fantasy world, like a bad villain, a villain creature." To me, his description illustrated his struggle with feeling "bad" and like a "villain." In contrast, Adam, an impulsive seven-year-old boy with severe attention deficit hyperactivity disorder, described the very same blot as "a design for something you wear or like a design for a toy you have. A design that would be on a toy because it looks like paint." As Adam's description centered on the use of paint, I was able to understand that he was struggling to organize his world and respond accurately to events. Adam sees events in an amorphous bloblike manner.

Another patient, Sarah, responded to the same card in a way that underscored her anxiety and avoidance of conflict, which helped me understand her school phobia. She said the card's image was "two people walking in separate directions. Two sisters in a fight who have not met for twenty years." As you can see, children come up with widely different and personalized responses to the cards that really help me enter their inner world.

Another personality test that helps me understand a child's emotional life is the Thematic Apperception Test (TAT). Students are given cards of pictures of people in ambiguous situations and asked to tell the story of what they see. Each card is loosely related to a specific theme. For example, a student may produce a story about an image of a boy looking at a violin. This story is usually connected with feelings about academic performance. The student then is asked to describe what the characters in the pictures are thinking, feeling, and doing. As evaluators, we are looking for the narrative, told by the student, to have a clear beginning, middle, and end. How children respond provides a window into understanding how well they resolve conflict and understand social relationships and the themes that preoccupy them.

In response to the picture of a boy with the violin, Ben, the highly anxious boy with academic challenges who described the Rorschach blot earlier, produced this story: "He is in a very boring music class, and he looks like he doesn't want to be there, but he is being forced by someone. He gets kicked out of class due to lack of attention." In this case, I can see Ben's feelings about being in class and fears of punishment very clearly. Sarah, an anxious, school-phobic tween who provided the Rorschach response earlier, produced this story in response to the same card: "He was playing violin, but it was too hard because he was trying to turn off the music thing without having lessons, so he gave up. He's feeling frustrated. No thoughts." When I asked Sarah if she thought the boy would play the violin again in the future, she said, "No." In this case, I could clearly see Sarah's avoidance of school-related tasks and her perception of academic difficulty in this story.

Understanding children's anxieties, fears, and concerns is vitally important to helping them emotionally and socially. The personality tests provide a valuable window into understanding how children feel about themselves and how they feel about school and their family so that we can pinpoint the most effective interventions.

Now you have a good understanding of the kind of testing that is done and what you can expect when your child is tested. But when should you have your child tested? You're not alone—many parents want to know when it is a good time to begin that process.

## WHEN TO TEST?

I always say that testing is indicated typically when a teacher or parent is concerned about a student's academic skills, social interactions, psychiatric symptoms, or behavioral concerns. I know this seems broad, because—let's face it—as parents, we are always concerned! But it's the truth and the best time. Trust your instinct. You know when your concern is more about your own anxiety or when you're accurately assessing your child's well-being. Sadly, parents are often ill-informed about the testing process and can feel confused, overwhelmed, and distressed. They may wonder, "What's wrong with my child? Is it my fault? Will my child be asked to leave his school? Will she ever be able to function in a normal environment?" But it absolutely doesn't have to be that way. A comprehensive assessment offers parents a window into their child's learning profile. Most importantly, if your child needs help, testing gets you started with an action plan to help.

A self-described "driven" father whom I'll call Jed recently consulted with me about his son, who he believed was "floundering" in a competitive academic environment. When Jed came to see me, he shared his frustration. He described his son as being temperamentally different from him. He told me that his son was more "relaxed," and Jed was concerned about his own life and the effect that his busy work as a lawyer might have on his relationship with his son. He was also worried about his son's depression and possible substance abuse. Clearly Jed loved his son. I presented testing as a way to potentially understand his son's academic and emotional struggles and suggested that this understanding might provide a means to improve the father-son relationship. Had I not invited Jed to share his concerns, he might have responded to the testing results by labeling or condemning his son in ways that would have undermined their relationship and his son's ability to thrive, both at home and in an academic environment.

The intake session provides a similar opportunity for a child to illuminate something about him- or herself that might otherwise be missed. These sessions are so important to building the type of rapport necessary for complete and accurate testing. Testing sounds impersonal but nothing could be further from the truth. Intakes can be used to build trust and help children become active inquirers, rather than passive subjects. Moreover, they set the stage for the feedback process by clarifying concerns about academic or social issues that can be addressed when discussing results.

My patient Andrew is a ten-year-old boy whose parents were concerned with his impulsivity at home and in school. Although a sweet boy, they told me he often interrupts others, gets extremely frustrated, and reacts aggressively. For example, he had recently pushed a classmate and threw his books on the ground. Andrew reported that his biggest concern was the bullying he was subjected to at school. When I questioned him further, he revealed that he had a lot of trouble with math and felt very distressed about how his parents, teachers, and peers thought he was "bad at math." He felt "stupid" and destined to be "friendless." I suggested we use the test results to help him understand his challenges with math and with making friends. His face lit up. He was enthusiastic about the possibility that the testing might help him have an easier time, both socially and academically.

## PREPARING YOUR CHILD FOR TESTING

Testing can be long; it typically takes two to three sessions lasting two to three hours each, wherein children are asked to perform boring and frustrating tasks. We also do a lot of tests that are similar to what they do in school, so many children can become irritated and feel uncomfortable with the demands of testing. In my practice, I create a positive experience for students despite these obvious drawbacks. I use several principles to make sure a child enjoys the testing and feels good about his or her performance. First, I collaborate with a student whenever possible. This means that I consult with them about scheduling, I ask their opinion about which test to administer first, I encourage them to speak up and let me know when they need a break, and I give them my complete attention. Most children appreciate the attention and enjoy chatting with me. Second, I carefully explain how the testing benefits them and reflects their individual experience. I find that young students completely appreciate the value of the testing. Because they buy into how they can be helped, their motivation and cooperation improve. Third, I incorporate fun elements into the testing. I play games with the kids, offer them snacks, and draw with them.

## INFORMATION GATHERING

I obtain a great deal of information from carefully listening to parents and children. But I don't stop there. I like to round out the picture by talking with the other people who spend time with students and really know them. Teachers are truly the "boots on the ground," and their knowledge of a student is an essential part of the testing process. I always speak with a student's school and often observe students at school to be sure I have the fullest picture of his or her academic life as possible. I use my discussions and observations as I prepare recommendations to help your child succeed academically. I also collaborate with the other professionals on your child's team, such as psychologists, psychiatrists, speech and language therapists, or physical therapists. My goal is to become part of the team, benefitting from their insights and sharing my test results to help them help your child.

An assessment of Eli, a preschool boy, revealed a bright, verbal child with significant distractibility and attentional difficulties. When I observed him in the classroom, I noted his engagement with his peers, his love for building, and his motivation to please his teachers. During conversations with the teachers and parents, I related my observation that he was one of the first children to comply with the direction to stop playing and go to the rug for circle time. He sat on the rug and assumed a yoga pose, apparently attempting to regulate and focus. Although he was only able to sit in the circle and attend to the teacher for the first ten minutes of the lesson, his motivation to please and to cooperate was impressive. Eli's teachers and parents enjoyed the anecdote and told me that he was a "good boy," despite his difficulty sustaining his focus on classroom routines and expectations. My observations about their son's behavior made his parents feel that I understood and was sympathetic toward their son. This greatly aided in their willingness to understand and accept the testing results.

## UNDERSTANDING THE NUMBERS

Test results are often understood in percentiles, so it is important to have a basic idea of statistics in order to properly interpret the results.

Evaluators compare your child with others his or her age using the bell curve. As you can see in figure 3.1, the curve is widest around the 50th percentile, because that is the average where most people are clustered.

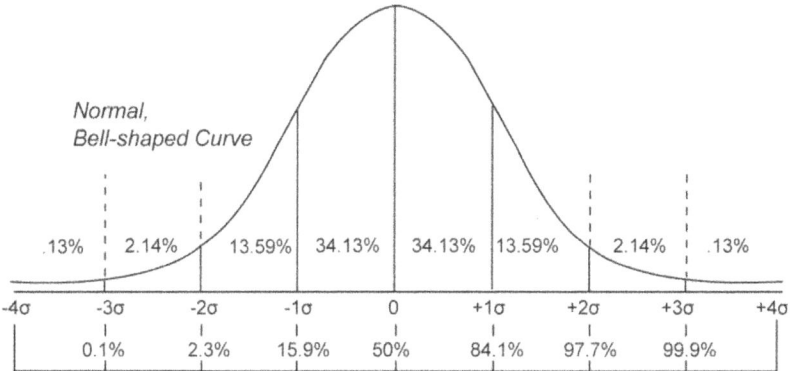

*Normal,*
*Bell-shaped Curve*

.13% | 2.14% | 13.59% | 34.13% | 34.13% | 13.59% | 2.14% | .13%

-4σ    -3σ    -2σ    -1σ    0    +1σ    +2σ    +3σ    +4σ

0.1%    2.3%    15.9%    50%    84.1%    97.7%    99.9%

**Figure 3.1.** Standard Bell Curve

In contrast, the tails are very small on both sides. So the majority of people function between the 25th and 75th percentile, whereas the outliers score in the 90th percentile or below the 25th. As you see in the examples presented, children with neurocognitive challenges vary wildly in their scores and often score on both sides of the curve: very high and very low. This is the definition of learning differences: they are not a flat line but rather zig and zag all over the place. It is important to keep that in mind when looking at your child's scores.

## DEFICITS ARE RELATIVE

Diagnosis is an important part of the testing process, as can be seen from the previous case examples. However, what is equally as important is a detailed and sophisticated analysis that compares the individual with his or her peers as well as identifying unique strengths and weaknesses within the individual's learning profile. When evaluating deficits, it is important to keep in mind that deficits are relative to the individual, and the goal of the neuropsychological evaluation is to create a comprehensive picture of the individual's neurocognitive strengths and weaknesses relative to him- or herself.

Likewise, it is important to note that having a learning disorder (LD) does not mean that the individual is not intelligent. Some children and adults with LD demonstrate superior IQ scores along with significant neurocognitive challenges. They're often referred to as "twice exceptional" because they are both intellectually gifted and learning disabled. When children are super-smart, their scores often are in the 90th to 99th percentile range, so you can see that an average score (50th percentile) represents an area of significant challenge and means that this student has either LD and/or ADHD.

Now that we understand the basics of testing, we delve into the typical neurocognitive profiles of children with LD, autism spectrum disorder, and ADHD.

## CHAPTER FOUR

# TESTING AND FEEDBACK WITH CHILDREN WITH ATTENTION DEFICIT HYPERACTIVITY DISORDER, LEARNING DISORDERS, AND AUTISM SPECTRUM DISORDER

In this chapter, I delve into the multifaceted world of children who are grappling with various learning disabilities. One of the best ways to do this is to offer a window into test reports, where we can see the important work of evaluators who illuminate the distinctive nuances of language-based learning disorders, dyslexia, nonverbal learning disorder, attention deficit disorder, and high-functioning autism. These snippets offer a vivid portrayal of the unique neuropsychological profiles defining each condition explored in preceding chapters. Beyond assessment, this chapter also covers neuropsychological feedback, the profound impact of diagnosis, and the pivotal role of effective communication within educational institutions. It's so important to understand and address these conditions, unveiling how diagnoses serve as guiding beacons in navigating the intricate realm of learning disabilities in children.

## LANGUAGE-BASED LEARNING DISORDER

As we know, the children who struggle with language-based learning disorders (LDs) have significant difficulty with expressing themselves and/or understanding others. Since communication is the building block for social and academic success, these children are truly at a severe disadvantage academically and socially. So what does their testing profile look like?

To start with, among those with language-based learning disabilities, verbal IQ is lower than visual-spatial IQ; these individuals do well with blocks, puzzles, and designs but often can't define words properly or express information about social situations. For example, I may ask a student with language-based learning issues a specific question such as, "What is the thing to do if you find someone else's wallet in a store?" A characteristic answer from someone who has trouble talking about social situations might be an overly vague response such as, "I would give it to my mom." This answer shows a lack of verbal sophistication, as they give an unelaborated, concrete response instead of saying, "I would look into the wallet to find the person's ID or hand the wallet to the store manager."

Among those with language-based LDs, visual memory is also significantly higher than their auditory memory, as these students can remember items presented to them visually but falter when asked to recall lists of words. Finally, they generally present academically with lowered reading and writing scores, as these skills are more language based.

Michael is an eight-year-old boy who was brought to me by his mother, Julia, who was concerned about his poor academic performance. Julia described Michael as a sweet, well-behaved boy who was not "getting it" when it came to reading and writing. I remember him telling me that math was "okay" and that he had a nice group of friends. To begin with, I assessed Michael's basic language abilities with select subtests from A Developmental Neuropsychological Assessment, second edition (NEPSY II), and Clinical Evaluation of Language Fundamentals, fourth edition (CELF-4), as well as the Peabody Picture Vocabulary Test, fourth edition (PPVT 4). These tests assess language-processing skills, which refer to a child's ability to "take in" information that is presented through language (receptive language) and to use language to express his or her understanding of an idea (expressive language). Scores on these tests can range from "very superior" (95th percentile) to "severely impaired" (5th percentile). According to his performance on the CELF-4, Michael's core language skills fall in the severely impaired range, meaning he is in the bottom percentile of language skills as compared with peers his age, a significant handicap, which explains why he is doing so poorly in school. Michael's expressive language skills were identified as his primary issue. He could not name most body parts, simple shapes, or produce words to describe varied experiences. Receptively, his comprehension was much better than his ability to express himself. He could identify pictures of common words by pointing, he easily followed simple directions, and could identify body parts. His profile of significant expressive language delays with improved receptive language skills is often found among children with language-based learning disabilities.

These findings guided his treatment and intervention, where I targeted his language skills and provided intervention for his challenges. I recommended Michael attend a special education school for children with language-based learning disabilities. In addition, I recommended he receive individual speech and language therapy in school. Michael attended this program and Julia told me happily that he was thriving academically.

In other words, understanding Michael's diagnostic profile provided a road map for targeted intervention. By addressing these specific deficits and leveraging his strengths, I set up interventions that empowered Michael's ability to navigate academic and social landscapes more effectively. It's this personalized approach that holds the promise for all students with learning issues to foster not just linguistic growth, but also to boost confidence and overall well-being as they progress in their personal and academic journeys.

## DYSLEXIA

Dyslexia is a specific reading disorder that is diagnosed when your child's reading skills fall significantly below average. Hallmarks of dyslexia include letter reversals, so your child may confuse *b* and *d*. Your child with dyslexia may also be unable to pair a letter with the correct sound, thus misreading and misspelling even simple words. What does the typical profile of a child with dyslexia look like? Reading skills are poor, both when asked to read silently and when asked to read aloud, auditory processing is often an area of challenge, and your child may also display visual spatial deficits; for example, have difficulty copying designs correctly. More specifically, we see the impact of compromised visual and auditory processing skills on reading acquisition. Sally, an eight-year-old girl, illustrates the typical performance of a child with dyslexia. When Sally's mother, Candace, first came to me, she described

Sally as a bubbly, social girl who had trouble focusing while in school. I knew that her difficulties across a range of reading skills was evidence of dyslexia. She struggled particularly with accuracy and decoding, and although, in some cases, she was able to understand passages by using context, she also had difficulties, to some extent, with comprehension. Sally attended a mainstream school and was receiving specialized academic support in a small-group setting every day in school.

Reading comprehension reflects one's ability to glean themes and detail from text. Sally's reading comprehension was generally stronger than her basic reading skills, which improved when she was able to refer back to what she read and review it more carefully or repeatedly. For the first test in this area, Sally was given a text to read and refer back to, which she was then asked questions about. Here, Sally scored in the upper end of the average range (WIAT-III, reading comprehension, standard score = 107, 67th percentile). However, on a similar test of reading comprehension for which she was asked to read aloud and was not permitted to refer back to the text while answering questions, Sally performed in the below average range (GORT, comprehension, scaled score = 7, 16th percentile). One clear difference between the two tests is that during the first test, she had the reading in front of her and could reread it. Another explanation may be the difference in retention between silent and out-loud reading. Sally may have been too focused on the decoding aspects of the reading when reading the passages in the GORT test, as this is an area of difficulty for her, which may have compromised her comprehension.

Sally's weaknesses in reading are particularly apparent in tasks of decoding and reading fluency, both of which measure her ability to understand the connection between letters and word sounds and articulate them smoothly, a task that integrates visual processing with auditory processing. On the first test that measured this skill, Sally was given a list of known words such as *they*, *cow*, and *when* and asked to read them aloud (WIAT-III, word reading, standard score = 100, 50th percentile, average). On this test, she was able to rely on her stored word knowledge and performed within the average range. However, on a nearly identical follow-up task, Sally was asked to read a list of nonsense words as if they were real words, thus relying entirely on phonemic processing.

Phonemic processing is the skill of sounding out words and knowing what the letters and vowels sound like. On this test, Sally struggled and often skipped words or stated existing words that contained similar letter combinations (WIAT-III, pseudoword decoding, standard score = 81, 23rd percentile, low average), elucidating Sally's significant struggles with reading. On additional tests of the GORT that measure reading fluency and accuracy, Sally demonstrated poor reading skills (GORT, reading fluency, scaled score = 7, 16th percentile, below average range; GORT, accuracy, Scaled Score = 6, 9th percentile, below average range). Even though Sally reads at an average rate, her skills are below average (GORT, reading rate, scaled score = 9, 37th percentile, average range). Together, these weaknesses point to difficulties in phonemic decoding and stringing words together fluidly.

Sally's reading abilities have been a focal point throughout her academic journey and both her teachers and mother have noted significant improvement due to her participation in small-group remediation. Though Sally attended these sessions before our diagnostic process, she still exhibited notable weaknesses in reading, fluency, and accuracy. After this comprehensive testing, I recommended that Sally attend a special education program designed for children with dyslexia. She transferred to this program, and I was delighted when her mother, Candace, told me that Sally had significantly improved her reading and writing skills.

## NONVERBAL LEARNING DISORDER

As described in chapter 2, children with a nonverbal learning disorder are extremely talkative and adept with words! However, they fall apart when presented with visual tasks, such as copying designs, putting together puzzles, and understanding maps. These issues have a ripple effect, not only negatively impacting their math skills, but so too their sense of direction and athletic ability. These students also suffer socially, as they don't understand body language and have trouble with social nuances. What does their neurocognitive profile look like?

Children with nonverbal learning disorder typically present with a high verbal IQ and a lower visual-spatial IQ. In addition, their ability to recall words is usually phenomenal, and yet strangely they can't recall details of pictures. Further, they typically work slowly and inaccurately when asked to copy designs or do any kind of pencil-and-paper task.

Here's an example from a wonderful patient of mine with a nonverbal learning disorder, on whose profile I shall focus on sections highlighting her visual delays. Charlotte is a poised and engaging fourteen-year-old girl who is doing well academically and socially. However, she suffers from severe anxiety because she has difficulty completing her work on time. She was referred for a reassessment by her mother to determine whether she meets criteria for accommodations. This example truly captures the significant impact of nonverbal learning disorder on developing visual skills. Ultimately, her disabilities met criteria for academic accommodations, including extra time and academic support.

Charlotte's cognitive abilities were assessed with the WISC-V, an individually administered test of a child's intellectual strengths and weaknesses in both verbal and nonverbal domains. Charlotte obtained a full-scale IQ score of 113 (81st percentile), indicating that her overall cognitive abilities fall within the high average range for her age. Her verbal comprehension index of 111 (77th percentile), fluid reasoning index of 118 (88th percentile), and working memory index of 110 (75th percentile) were also high average, while her processing speed index of 103 (58th percentile) was average. However, Charlotte's visual-spatial reasoning index of 86 (18th percentile) fell within the low average range and was significantly lower than her other verbal and visual abilities and reflects an area of neurocognitive weakness related to continued difficulties associated with her nonverbal learning disorder.

Charlotte's verbal abilities are strong for her age, as she demonstrated a high average ability to understand verbal information and provide verbal responses. She performed in the high average range when asked to articulate the definitions of words, reflecting an excellent ability to learn and recall information from long-term memory. Charlotte's conceptual verbal reasoning abilities were also well-developed and fell at the top of the average range when asked to describe the similarities between words.

Charlotte's perceptual reasoning abilities, which include her nonverbal reasoning and visual-spatial skills, were highly variable. She demonstrated extremely high abstract visual problem-solving abilities on an untimed task that required her to analyze and complete visual patterns based on color, form, and distribution in space. However, her performance on timed nonverbal tasks was significantly lower and reflects her slowed speed when working with complex visual material. Her quantitative reasoning abilities fell within the average range when asked to identify the correct number and types of weights to keep scales balanced. Charlotte's visual-spatial reasoning skills fell within the low average when required to re-create graphic designs with colored blocks and identify the components of visual puzzles. Notably, Charlotte lost credit across all three timed visual reasoning tasks by answering items correctly outside of testing time limits, indicating that her potential is higher when given additional time.

Charlotte's working memory abilities, which refer to the ability to store and manipulate information in short-term memory, were also variable. Her verbal working memory skills were very high when reciting strings of numerals verbatim and in reverse and numerical order. However, her visual working memory abilities were significantly lower on a task that required her to identify pictures of objects previously studied for five seconds, again reflecting her slowed speed on complex visual tasks.

Processing speed is a measure of psychomotor ability, which is the capacity to process simple or routine information fluently and automatically. Charlotte's graphomotor speed was high average when copying shapes paired with numbers. However, her visual scanning and discrimination abilities were significantly lower when asked to identify matching or nonmatching abstract symbol groups.

In sum, Charlotte is a very bright and capable girl with excellent academic potential. She demonstrated a sophisticated vocabulary, reflecting a very strong ability to learn and recall information from long-term memory. In addition, her abstract visual problem-solving skills were excellent. However, Charlotte's performance on timed nonverbal tasks was significantly compromised by her slowed speed when working with complex visual information, reflecting her nonverbal learning disorder.

I recommended that Charlotte receive extended time on tests and assignments in school. This recommendation was welcomed enthusiastically by Charlotte and really helped relieve her anxiety about test taking and improve her scores significantly. I also recommended that Charlotte work with an executive functioning coach to help her organize, plan out her assignments, and submit her assignments on time. Charlotte began working with a coach and her assignment record improved!

## ATTENTION DEFICIT DISORDER

As mentioned in chapter 1, children with attention deficit disorder (ADD) have real trouble focusing. They tend to run around a lot, get distracted easily, and are usually quite jumpy. They also may "space out," be very disorganized, be forgetful, and impulsively ignore rules. In addition, their memory is often erratic because they "tune out" and their speed is slow because they get distracted. As you can imagine, these behaviors can be very problematic in school, at home, and with friends. In order to diagnose ADD, there are specific attention tests that we discussed in chapter 3. Your child must meet criteria for these tests to have a diagnosis.

Darlene is a fourteen-year-old girl who often gets in trouble for her impulsivity and fidgety behaviors. She was referred to me by her mother, Ms. S., to assess her attention and provide recommendations for intervention.

I first assessed Darlene with the Conners Continuous Performance Test, third edition (CPT-III), to assess her attention abilities. This fourteen-minute target decision task requires the respondent to press the space bar as letters are presented on a computer screen. The individual is further instructed not to press the space bar when the letter $X$ is presented. Although Darlene made an age-appropriate number of errors, her response speed slowed over the course of the task, indicating reduced attention over time.

Darlene's attention and executive functioning were also assessed on the BASC-3, a behavioral rating scale for children and adolescents, which includes both parent and self-reports. Her responses indicated that she experienced significant difficulties with inattention and hyperactivity. For example, Darlene reported that she almost always has a hard time concentrating and that she often has trouble paying attention to the teacher, is easily distracted, and forgets to do things. Further, she also almost always has trouble sitting still and feels like she has to get up and move around. Darlene's responses also revealed impulsivity, as she explained, for example, that she almost always talks while other people are talking and that she talks without waiting for others to say something. Darlene's mother's responses also detailed her heightened hyperactivity and impulsivity. For example, Ms. S. indicated that Darlene almost always interrupts others when they are speaking, talks over others, sometimes acts without thinking, and cannot wait to take a turn.

In sum, Darlene's performance on attention and executive functioning assessments indicated mild attention deficits and heightened hyperactivity and impulsivity, consistent with her diagnosis of attention deficit hyperactivity disorder. I recommended that Darlene consult with a psychiatrist to receive stimulants to help improve her attention and focus and reduce impulsivity. In addition, I recommended that Darlene consult with a therapist to help her better understand social situations and teach her techniques so she can conform to behavioral norms. Happily, Darlene began working with a therapist and taking medication. A follow-up six months later revealed that Darlene was a "different child" who was significantly less impulsive and no longer got into trouble at school or with friends.

## HIGH-FUNCTIONING AUTISM

The child who is on the autism spectrum typically has a host of neuro-cognitive challenges that impact his or her ability to succeed academically and socially. Intellectually, your child is usually highly intelligent but can be very rigid and take things literally. For example, despite an excellent vocabulary, he or she may not be able to define proverbs such as "one swallow does not make a summer" or use inferential reasoning to figure out a solution to a problem. Interestingly, they typically can recall details perfectly but may miss the main point of a story, as they have trouble with inferences and get stuck on extraneous details. For example, when given a passage about a little boy who gets lost, they can go into great detail about the appearance of the boy but cannot infer that he was scared about being lost. In order to make sure that a diagnosis of autism is correct, your child must score significantly on certain tests specific to autism, which were discussed in chapter 3.

Harold is a five-year-old boy who was referred for testing by his parents due to continued concerns regarding his social/emotional, language, and behavioral development. His mother reported that although Harold met all developmental milestones within expected limits as an infant, at the age of one, he began exhibiting language and social/emotional delays. For example, he did not respond to his name; he walked on tiptoes; he engaged in repetitive and/or obsessive behaviors, such as opening and closing doors; and he developed heightened sensory sensitivities to textures and foods.

Harold talks at length about topics that interest him and therefore is unable to maintain friendships and proper social interactions. His frustration tolerance is very low, and he has trouble managing transitions, following directions, and waiting for his turn. Further, he demonstrates perfectionistic tendencies; for example, if he colors outside of lines or otherwise makes mistakes while drawing, he quickly tantrums. Harold is also very interested in video games, Pokémon, and animals, and his mother reports that he loves books and learning and has a strong vocabulary. He has a good sense of humor and can be very funny, and despite his social difficulties, he demonstrates interest in his peers and would like to develop friendships.

Harold's history of social and emotional difficulties was evident on social/emotional and personality testing. On the Autism Spectrum Rating Scales (ASRS), his mother indicated that Harold has difficulty using verbal and nonverbal communication appropriately to initiate, engage in, and maintain social contact and has limited capacity to successfully engage in activities that develop and maintain relationships with other children and adults. In addition, Harold has significant difficulty tolerating changes in his environment, routines, activities, or behaviors, and has elevated sensitivity to sensory input. Overall, these behaviors align with *The Diagnostic and Statistical Manual of Mental Disorders*, fifth edition (DSM-5), criteria for autism spectrum disorder. Further, on the ADOS-2, which is a semi-structured play and observational assessment, Harold's overall score indicated a moderate level of autism-related symptoms. Although he was very sociable and interested in talking to the examiner, demonstrating good eye contact and the ability to make social overtures and hold joint attention, Harold exhibited stereotypic language, misuse of semantics and grammar, restricted interest, behavioral rigidity, and hand flapping when excited.

These social difficulties appear to have led to heightened feelings of anxiety and depression. His mother indicated on the BASC-3 that Harold frequently displays behaviors stemming from worry, nervousness, and/or fear and that he is at times withdrawn, pessimistic, and sad. Harold becomes easily overwhelmed by these emotions and has difficulty controlling his behavior and recovering when faced with changes or challenges.

In sum, results of social/emotional and personality testing indicate that Harold exhibits impairments in his social communication and interaction as well as heightened rigidity that reflect a diagnosis of autism spectrum disorder. He also demonstrates significant feelings of anxiety and sadness. Psychotherapy was recommended along with placement in a small, structured class setting to accommodate Harold's behaviors and help him flourish academically and socially.

As can be seen, diagnosing high-functioning autism is complicated and requires attention to multiple factors including self-report, family observations, and performance on tests. Now that we understand the typical neurocognitive profile of children with a variety of issues let's discuss what happens once the testing has been completed.

## NEUROPSYCHOLOGICAL FEEDBACK

Once testing is complete, the important step of giving feedback to parents is next. Parents should always be the first to receive feedback to ensure they understand the results. After you receive feedback, your child should also receive his or her own specific feedback session to help them understand how they learn and function in the world. A good tester presents an action plan and collaborates with you on figuring out how to access the resources and services that they recommend. Often, it is a good idea to consult with your child's school and explain the findings to the teachers. In addition, as accommodations are often recommended, a careful review of these school-based interventions helps set up your child for success. It is also very important to discuss the results with all professionals working with your child so that they fully understand the findings and can treat him or her collaboratively and effectively.

Let me introduce Alex, a shy, sweet thirteen-year-old boy, to illustrate how feedback helps everyone, including the school, take the necessary steps to ensure a student's success.

Alex was brought in by his parents because they were concerned about his erratic grades; he did really well in math but often faltered when presented with English and history tests. He complained of losing focus, running out of time, and being unable to double-check his work. Marcia, his mother, explained that he was a snuggly boy who was teased by his older brother and often retaliated by punching him or erupting in angry outbursts. Alex shared with me that he wanted to do well in school but worried because he could not finish his tests. He felt that reading was a chore and revealed that sometimes he didn't understand directions or classroom information. He denied feeling distressed about his brother and said they were good friends.

When I met with Alex and his parents, I explained that Alex had a language-based learning disorder and often did not comprehend reading material and tended to read slowly and laboriously. In addition, he was a genius at math and scored exceptionally high on tasks, tapping his ability to complete puzzles and use his analytic skills. Alex was extremely pleased with these results. He smiled upon hearing how smart he was and clearly resonated with having difficulty with words as well as reading and writing. I recommended extra time on tests, meeting with a learning specialist to get academic support, as well as psychotherapy. Critical to his success, I consulted with the school staff, and they were happy to put these recommendations in place. Alex expressed relief and optimism about his academic future.

Feedback can be a transformative experience for everyone involved, but it can also bring up distressing feelings. Parents and children can feel embarrassed about their child's challenges and distressed by the recommendations. It is important to get support and realize you are not alone on this journey. When the tester is able to carefully explain what is going on with the child and give valuable recommendations, parents and children start to relax and feel optimistic about the future.

Another example is my patient Sarah, an eleventh grader, who came to me for performance anxiety about her schoolwork, which manifested in her avoiding her work, "spacing out," and becoming easily frustrated.

My evaluation of her revealed significant attentional deficits. Feedback with Sarah's parents, Bob and Sue, focused on explaining that she has difficulty focusing, sitting and focusing on her work, and completing tasks in an efficient manner. In their presence, Sarah confirmed that she is easily distracted and procrastinates. As Bob and Sue began to understand that they had misinterpreted her attentional deficits as anxiety, their concerns were reassured, and they arranged to consult with a psychopharmacologist for medicine for Sarah. Understanding Sarah's specific symptoms of ADD made it a lot easier to tolerate and intervene effectively.

## REACTIONS TO DIAGNOSIS

Parents can often feel angry that they did not receive the proper diagnosis earlier and frustrated that they "wasted" time with ineffective interventions. Julia, a successful lawyer, was astounded that the experts in her daughter's world never had an inkling that her daughter was suffering from a learning disorder. "Why didn't the pediatrician and the school realize my daughter is dyslexic?" She was irate that her eight-year-old daughter's reading challenges could have been addressed far earlier, something that would have been so much better, and importantly easier, for her daughter.

Parents often feel shame that their child has neurocognitive challenges. As parents, we often feel that our child's accomplishments and failures reflect either how well or how poorly we have done as parents. Having a child with special needs can be a tough pill to swallow. As mentioned, it is essential to get support from the community, friends, and professionals. Feelings of guilt can also take over, as many parents lament their previous reactions to their child's challenges. I often hear parents regretfully remember how hard they came down on their children. "If only they had known" is a common refrain. Other parents realize that they have harbored unrealistic expectations or blamed their children for their neurocognitive challenges. It can be a painful reckoning for all involved.

Sometimes parents too can feel anxious about the results and worry that a diagnosis or accommodations will make the situation worse, not better. Parents will say, "They don't get extended time in the real world!" They're concerned that their child won't be able to function without special services. Others feel that if their children receive tutoring or homework help, they will lose their independence, feeling that it's "cheating" as "they are not doing the work themselves." If psychopharmacological intervention is recommended, some parents who are opposed to medication worry about the side effects. A central goal in my practice is to help parents understand that their child has real difficulties and needs help. I often use the analogy of a child with poor eyesight who needs glasses. I further explain that the services and accommodations are designed to level the playing field, helping their child function up to his or her potential.

For many parents, their child's diagnosis comes as a relief. On more than one occasion, I worked with parents who exclaimed, "I knew something was wrong, but nobody could tell me what it was." As Michal, a nutritionist reported, "You explained to me what was wrong with my son; now I understand how to help him and will never give up until he succeeds." The diagnosis and feedback can be reenergizing and clarifying, giving hope and a clear action plan. Parents can now understand and empathize with their child and come up with the correct way to help him or her. Interestingly, many parents identify their own learning challenges as a result of the testing and quite a few ask to be tested themselves as they see how helpful it has been for their children.

## COMMUNICATION WITH THE SCHOOL: HOW DIAGNOSIS HELPS

Once a proper diagnosis has been identified, we can intervene appropriately and understand what is going on with your child. This information can be communicated to the teachers and school administration so they can also work effectively with your student. The following example illustrates how "knowledge is power" and understanding the child is the key to helping them.

Richard was a ten-year-old boy who frequently wandered out of his classroom to complain to the principal about somatic or emotional concerns. He would tearfully describe having stomachaches and headaches.

Sadly, the principal referred to the behavior as "manipulative." However, comprehensive testing revealed that Richard was missing basic writing skills; he was simply leaving the classroom to evade the profound embarrassment of struggling with these tasks. I explained to his parents and school personnel that, as a result of his learning difficulties, Richard was becoming overloaded and disorganized when presented with challenging work. I recommended several strategies, including the use of an iPad, dictation devices, and instructor-based support to help him with his writing issues—which, of course, indirectly helped quell his disruptive behavior. The teacher incorporated these techniques, and the wandering behaviors subsided. A solution can be that simple, yet the transformation is life changing.

Feedback can be communicated to school personnel in face-to-face meetings, phone consultations, and via email; each modality requires different skills. The guiding principles, however, remain the same: to address the questions and concerns that professionals have about the student, to explicate the test data, and to provide clear recommendations for intervention. Good testers are always mindful that other team members may have different perspectives about the student and therefore need to find a way to communicate the test results both effectively and respectfully, always in the student's best interest.

My assessment of Jason, a soft-spoken, athletic nine-year-old boy, revealed impaired reading comprehension due to an overly concrete and rigid learning style. Jason arrived in my office with a worried expression and fidgety behaviors, such as jiggling his leg and leaping up from his chair. For Jason's success, I suggested a team approach that included a specialized reading tutor, clinical therapy, and psychotropic medication, as well as small-group instruction in school. Of note, our team of parents, teachers, and school administrators convened at the end of the school year to discuss Jason's progress and recommendations for the fall. During the meeting, multiple members of the team voiced confusion about Jason's erratic behavior and reading skills. One teacher offered the following observation: "He can't work independently, and he can only finish a project when I'm sitting with him." She felt this behavior was emotional and manipulative. It was important to keep my eye on the prize, which was Jason's best interest. I made a point to be her ally, stating that I agreed that Jason was anxious and impulsive. I complimented her on her ability to be supportive and reassuring. I then explained that Jason was not deliberately causing trouble or being overly demanding. Rather, his behaviors were the result of his neurocognitive difficulties; he had great difficulty organizing his thoughts, extrapolating information, and making inferences. He was able to work better with the teacher because he was able to read important cues from her that compensated for his areas of difficulty. I explained how she was acting as a scaffold—that is, giving him sequential cues as she sat with him—and how he benefited from this structure. These insights facilitated a deeper understanding of his learning style and improved her ability to work effectively with him.

Testers should always check in with parents to ensure that they understand the feedback of the test results and how it applies to family and school life. For example, children with ADHD often have trouble complying with household responsibilities and routines, such as doing chores or brushing their teeth. When parents understand that their children are not being "bad" or "lazy," they can figure out how to help their children accomplish these tasks successfully.

Neuropsychological feedback is pivotal for parents to receive vital insights about their child's cognitive functions after testing. It ensures parents have a clear understanding of the results before the child receives his or her equally important tailored feedback session. Collaborating on an action plan, including recommended resources and accommodations, forms a core part of this process. Engaging with your child's school and all professionals to ensure a cohesive approach is crucial. Most parents are relieved but even among those parents who experience distress, this feedback offers invaluable guidance and optimism for their child's academic future, bridging understanding and offering support and a clear pathway for the whole family.

## CHAPTER FIVE

# SUPPORTING NEURODIVERSE CHILDREN AT HOME AND IN THE CLASSROOM

Supporting and rooting for our children as students is one of the cornerstones of great parenting. Now that we understand your child's diagnosis and his or her unique profile of strengths and challenges, let's consider how this knowledge can facilitate his or her success. Consider how difficult and frustrating it is to be a young person with neurocognitive challenges. They feel hurt, bewildered, and "out of step" with their peers. In addition, they often face crushing disapproval from parents and teachers, as they have difficulty complying with expectations both large and small. Though you, as parent or educator, may struggle with your youngsters yourself, you may be surprised to learn that they are hardest on themselves.

The most detrimental aspect for these children is the internal struggle of self-blame and self-loathing, wherein they perceive themselves as "damaged goods," "lazy," "stupid," and "defective." There's no doubt that trying to work with a child with these types of challenges can feel overwhelming. Parents and educators often have similar feelings as those of their child or student: frustration, anger, confusion, sadness, hurt, and a lack of connection with each other. It's almost a mirror, but the origins of all of these uncomfortable feelings come from very different places.

For adults, the challenge lies in the uncertainty of understanding the true nature of the situation. Is it a genuine incapability? Or is it a matter of being perceived as bratty or lazy? Could it be rooted in emotional factors, neurological issues, or perhaps a combination of both? Crucially, parents find themselves pondering: "Where can we find the help we need?"

What's important to remember is that when parents and teachers blame children for their failings, it creates a vicious cycle in which children blame and feel terrible about themselves and continue to fail;

eventually they simply withdraw from the tasks entirely. On the other hand, parents and teachers can work from a strengths-based and empathic perspective, offering a valuable and gentle understanding that undoubtedly improves a child's confidence and abilities. It sounds almost too simple, but your own awareness can help your child recover and restore his or her sense of self. In this chapter, I review common responses to neurodivergence and offer suggestions to help your child thrive and flourish at home and in school.

You can start helping your child by understanding the parallel process that exists between you—the parent or teacher—and your child/student. As stated earlier, the feelings of all stakeholders in this circumstance reflect each other, leading to a complex interaction that either can facilitate success or contribute to failure. In other words, you hold an important key to your child's outcome.

Children flourish when they feel confident and supported; sadly, neurodivergence often leaves children feeling terribly anxious about their skills and criticized by the adults who are most important in their world. Faced with this potent and toxic mix, children withdraw, lie, express defiance, and act aggressively. The adults around them then react to these behaviors often punitively, further exacerbating their child's low self-worth and feelings of failure.

We live in a pressure cooker, where there is enormous focus on success and failure, which is defined in a very narrow way. Success means a child who excels academically, socially, and athletically. Parents go to great lengths to ensure that their child gets into the "right school" and has the "right connections," viewing this as a checklist for vicarious pride. Having a neurodivergent child who may need to go to a special education school and has multiple challenges in different arenas, including on the playing field, at parties, and in school, can be exquisitely painful and humiliating. Think about those parents who bribed colleges to get their children into Ivy League schools. Our culture imposes the narrative that getting your child into an Ivy is the ticket to success. No wonder parents are so stressed about their children!

Shame is a fascinating emotion that functions as a "hot potato" and gets passed back and forth among family members. For example, a father feels humiliated by his boss's criticism of him at work, so he comes home and shames his wife about her lousy cooking. Along those lines, a child might feel embarrassed by his poor grade on a test, so he comes home and bullies his younger brother about being a "baby." Parents transmit their own feelings of shame and inadequacy, creating these feelings in their children, further contributing to a proclivity of avoidance in both social and academic spheres. In wonderful contrast, nurturing feelings of appreciation and gratitude play a pivotal role in cultivating a sense of self-acceptance and confidence in children. By highlighting children's strengths and acknowledging their progress, parents contribute significantly to their children's ability to discern and embrace their own resilience and perseverance.

## COMMON TEACHER AND PARENT REACTIONS

Teacher and parent reactions range from unconcerned and negligent to punitive and overly involved. And because neurocognitive challenges are often misdiagnosed, overlooked, and mislabeled, parents and teachers may not understand what is going on with their child and thus may overreact or underreact, depending on their thoughts about the situation. For example, a fidgety child's restlessness, who in fact suffers from ADD, may be misinterpreted as defiant; instead of recognized as neurodiverse, he or she is subject to disciplinary action and told to stay inside for recess. To make matters worse, because they don't understand the etiology of their difficulties, such children often react with frustration, avoidance, procrastination, and defiance, furthering a negative cycle of interactions with authority figures and peers. The cycle begins with an undiagnosed, neurocognitively challenged child struggling with a task and missing the mark in terms of adult expectations.

Here's an example of a young patient of mine. Sally cannot complete a math worksheet. She looks around and sees her peers racing confidently through the sheet, and she is stuck. At this point, Sally gets frustrated, stressed, overwhelmed, and disappointed with herself. In reaction, she pushes the sheet away and puts her head on the desk. The teacher then reprimands her and orders her to "keep working." She dutifully picks up her pencil but once again is stymied by the questions. Again, she pushes the worksheet away and loudly announces that she doesn't want to do this "stupid sheet." She is feeling so frustrated and angry by this point that she starts to cry. Her classmates are bewildered by her outburst and snicker as her teacher marches to her desk and yells at her, "Why do you think you can act this way? You are being really disruptive." Sally puts her head down on her desk to block out the mocking jeers and the hurtful reprimand of her teacher. She wishes the floor would swallow her up; she would rather be anywhere in the world than in her own skin in this classroom.

But Sally didn't have to suffer. In an ideal scenario, a supportive and understanding approach from both parents and teachers could make a significant difference. By offering consistent support and scaffolding, adults can empower children like Sally to advocate for themselves, fostering a more inclusive and nurturing learning environment. As a clinician who is a staunch advocate for patients with neurodiversity, it is heartbreaking to see this and similar narratives played out again and again, year after year, in my practice. It is essential to recognize and address the unique needs of children, making certain that no student endures the emotional turmoil that Sally faced in the classroom.

My years of experience with patients have given me an inside view of families of all kinds. I've met a variety of parents, all of whom care deeply for their children and very much want success and happiness for them. However, some parents don't understand that they fall into very clear boxes of helpfulness and hurtfulness when it comes to their children with neurocognitive challenges. Let's take a look.

## THE DEMANDING DAD

I first met Leslie when she was in seventh grade. A precocious, pretty, and engaging girl with a shy smile and glasses, she was characterized by her peers as a definite "nerd." Leslie was drawn to intellectual and somewhat isolating experiences. She loved spending quiet time with her dog and even at a young age spent time at art museums pondering the historical nature of paintings. She went to the theater with her mother, drawn to the rich and complex narratives of playwrights. She also educated herself on YouTube, learning about art history and Jewish culture. As bright and energetic as she was, Leslie had serious difficulty completing assignments; she recounted how she wanted to curl into a ball and kick and scream, anything other than do her work. In fact, she often did not complete her assignments. Although Leslie had a learning disorder (LD), she attended a mainstream elementary school and then later a special education high school. One of her most painful childhood memories was going to the bookstore with her dad and asking him to buy her picture books, only to be told that these were for babies and that she needed to read chapter books instead. Her father also expected her to complete homework assignments independently, despite her need for support academically. These demands and expectations only escalated as she got older. Despite Leslie's established diagnosis, placement in a special ed high school, and psychoeducation administered by professionals, Leslie's father continued to insist that she was "lazy" and did not have an LD. This created significant anxiety and caused Leslie to internalize a false belief that she was "stupid." This poignant situation underscores the immense influence a parent's opinion can wield, shaping not only a child's self-perception but also impacting his or her journey with learning differences. It serves as a powerful reminder of the importance of empathy, understanding, and validation in a child's educational and emotional development.

## THE MICROMANAGER

Sean, an athletic, handsome teenager who achieved straight As at an extremely competitive private school, harbored guilty secrets: he had never completed reading a book and his father wrote the final drafts of his papers for him. Although Sean was incredibly conscientious and hardworking, his undiagnosed dyslexia prevented him from reading at an appropriate pace. He compensated by skimming books but never reading them from cover to cover. His father micromanaged his work, especially his papers. Although Sean would write the paper, his father would then completely edit, thoroughly revising and even providing new, snappy titles. The result: Sean grew up feeling like a fraud and an imposter, eroding his confidence and the opportunity for self-expression. Although Sean's father's motives were well-intentioned, they had a devastating effect on Sean's personal sense of adequacy.

## MISMATCHED AT SCHOOL

Olive, a twelve-year-old girl with long, blonde hair and sparkling blue eyes, came to me for testing due to concerns about her erratic grades, which seemed to be on a roller coaster. Despite excelling at advanced classes at school and actively participating in discussions, Olive was grappling with anxiety over her academic performance. Even with the added support of private tutoring at home, poor test scores left her visibly distressed. At home, there was a challenge as well: trying to tackle homework in her bedroom led to conflicts with her mother. Olive's insecurities about her skills added an extra layer of difficulty to the situation. It's a complex scenario for a young student who needs to navigate both academic and emotional pressures.

My assessment of Olive revealed LD, particularly in math. She was thrilled when I immediately recommended that she attend regular math instead of advanced math. She enthusiastically designed her own schedule to accommodate her learning challenges. But when I presented this idea to school staff, they were reluctant; despite her very poor grades, Olive participated in class, asked questions, and seemed on top of her classwork—in their minds, she was "holding her own." I explained that Olive is highly verbal and very comfortable with ideas but can't execute the problems. The school finally agreed. Olive moved down a notch in math and immediately started excelling and feeling confident about her academic skills. This newfound confidence created a positive cycle in which Olive approached her work enthusiastically, was able to complete all the assignments on time, and her mood improved.

## HELPFUL

Parents desperately want to help a child who is suffering, but help comes in many different forms. Parents who observe, monitor, support, and answer questions are far more helpful than those who take over homework because they can't tolerate seeing their child struggle. In recent years, there's been a noticeable shift in parenting dynamics. The need to shield one's child from struggle seems particularly strong in today's world. This could be due to increased competitiveness in education or even the social media pressures placed on children and families. When parents provide all the answers for children or write their essays for them, the children gain the impression that they are not capable of doing the work; they become overly dependent on their parents. Additionally, teachers lose the opportunity to accurately evaluate their students' skills. From an education perspective, it is far better for students to hand in substandard homework than to hand in a correct exercise that they did not do. This can be excruciating for both parent and child; the student begs the parent to give him or her the answers, and the parent just wants to help. It's essential for adults to understand the difference between supporting and intervening.

## HURTFUL

Providing incentives or deterrents as a strategy for motivating children with neurocognitive disorders does not address the root causes of their challenges. For example, it is both detrimental and inadequate to promise children additional screen time or a present if they do their work or receive good grades or, conversely, to punish them for poor grades or incomplete homework. Using external measures to address the problem doesn't work because the issues are internal and rooted in neurocognitive/psychiatric issues. With parents, I often use the analogy of an "invisible wheelchair" to emphasize that you wouldn't threaten a child in a wheelchair to "walk or else!" Children with neurocognitive disorders require understanding, support, and specialized interventions tailored to their unique needs. They do not need punitive or incentive-based approaches.

## THE YELLER

In my practice, I have seen parents with a damaging pattern of stern admonishment and chastisement. Alice, in her forties, tearfully recounted the challenges she faces raising her six-year-old Kate who, while bubbly and imaginative, cannot control her voice, temper, and body impulses. Frequently reprimanded by her mother and teachers, Kate has tremendous difficulty adhering to very simple rules and expectations. Alice, feeling intensely frustrated, often yells at Kate, causing her to cry, run to her room, and write apology notes. Alice's interventions have no positive impact on Kate's behavior; she continues to yell, hit her brother, and ignore directions and expectations. Kate's behavior at school is also concerning, showing similar challenges with listening to directions. Although reminded multiple times not to dawdle during PE, Kate stops to pick up a flower, seemingly completely bewildered as to why she is in trouble. At bedtime she confides to her mother that she forgets the rules but has such an overwhelming surge of energy that she wants to do cartwheels. She adds that she doesn't enjoy school and is bored and unhappy in the mornings.

When I advised Alice to write down three positive expectations for Kate, she shared the following: (1) using her indoor voice; (2) playing nicely with her brother; and (3) helping with her younger sister. I suggested that when Kate fails to meet these expectations, Alice should calmly say, "Kate you are a good girl, but you are having difficulty listening right now; let's work together and mom will help you." The "good girl" message should be amplified throughout the day. A follow-up phone call revealed that these strategies had a dramatic impact on Kate's behavior. She was relaxed, happy, and confident at home, and mother and daughter were able to have a great weekend together.

The best way for parents and teachers to help students with neuro-cognitive disorders is to get help from an expert. Neuropsychologists are trained in the assessment of children with learning, attention, and emotional differences. Understanding the nuances of your child's learning style will help guide your response to their challenges. Neuropsychologists function much like investigators, delving into the mysteries behind why your child is struggling with school, friendships, or behaviors. We do that by administering a compendium of tests (as discussed in chapter 3) designed to figure out the specific strengths and challenges your child presents.

Now that we understand your child's learning profile and emotional makeup, how do we put this valuable information into practice?

## DIAGNOSIS LEADS TO UNDERSTANDING AND IMPROVED PARENTING

Melissa came to my office with concerns about her son Jacob, who was reluctant to try new foods and activities and could not tolerate any breaks in his routine. His test results indicated that he met diagnostic criteria for autism spectrum disorder (ASD). This was a boy who navigated the world with an excessively rigid mindset, a concrete understanding of language, and who struggled with adapting to change. After I explained the etiology of his difficulties, Melissa was able to work more effectively with Jacob when preparing him for change and began to better regulate her reactions when he expressed difficulty with transitions. Knowing her son had neurocognitive impairments helped her move away from the assertion that he was merely a "brat." She began to empathize with him and intervene more effectively when he was having trouble.

Let's explore the impact of a child's issues on family life. First, children with attention deficit hyperactivity disorder (ADHD) often have trouble complying with household chores and routines. Parents with these kids often complain that they do everything slowly and can't get it together to leave the house on time. When parents can intellectualize that the slowed speed is neurocognitive in nature, they can then begin to brainstorm strategies that facilitate these transitions. For example, using a whiteboard with a checklist of "to-do" items can jog the child's memory and eliminate the need to repeat directives each and every morning. This can lead to a more relaxed start to the day. Giving directions one step at a time is essential for children with attention deficit disorder (ADD); if you give them too many steps to complete, they get lost and are unable to perform the task. For example, instead of saying "clean up the living room," a mindful parent might say, "Please take all the papers on the floor and throw them into the garbage." This ensures cooperation.

## CATCH THEM BEING GOOD

My work with neurodivergent children isn't just professional; it's personal. My seventeen-year-old daughter Renee, who is also dyslexic, recently told me about a study in a Romanian orphanage where they divided children into two groups: one received positive reinforcement such as compliments, hugs, stars, and tokens, whereas the other group received negative responses such as yelling, removal of privileges, time out, and criticism. As they matured, there were stark differences between the two groups, with the positive reinforcement group outstripping the negative group in every sphere: social, academic, emotional, and behavioral. This story struck me as apocryphal, but the lesson was clear. All children flourish and thrive when presented with opportunities to succeed and please the adults around them. Children with neurocognitive challenges struggle more than most to conform to behavioral rules, succeed academically, or progress emotionally. Thus, it is essential that parents and teachers practice positive reinforcement at every opportunity. In this way, all children, including those with neurocognitive issues, can not only thrive, but also build a foundation for lifelong success and well-being.

## HELPFUL

My advice from years of clinical practice is to unearth your child's passion and encourage it. Help them discover their strengths and reinforce those skills with exposure and practice. For example, many children with dyslexia are very visual and creative. Taking them to museums, enrolling them in art classes, and setting up an art space at home can foster these skills. In addition, recognizing the gains they are making as they struggle is very important to convey. Parents need to show their understanding and appreciation for their neurodiverse children and the efforts they make. Make a point of complimenting your child every day on some achievement, whether it is cooking a meal, doing their homework, or coming up with a good joke.

## HURTFUL

Amid the intricate tapestry of parenting, it can be particularly harmful for parents of neurodivergent children to succumb to the inclination of comparing their kids to neurotypical counterparts. Such comparison isn't only emotionally taxing, but also counterproductive. What may seem effortlessly achievable to others can present as near insurmountable challenges for these children, which is why there is such a critical need for parents to emphasize empathy, understanding, and acceptance rather than comparison. The sooner you recognize that your child is on his or her own unique journey, the better off both of you will be.

My clinical meeting with the family of a twenty-year-old young man diagnosed with dyslexia and ADD poignantly illustrates the effects of this type of parent reaction. Possessed of a sweet disposition, Alan arrived at my office having struggled his entire academic career due to undiagnosed learning and attention issues. At home, his father was a yeller who often expressed his frustration by screaming at Alan that he was "lazy, missed deadlines," and was not performing on par with the children of his friends. This need to "keep up with the Joneses" was totally detrimental to his son. Recently, Alan was taking two online classes. He was completing all of his work and engaged in the material. For the first week he was doing quite well, and it marked the first time in his academic career that he had ever been able to do this. Alan's parents were pleased but then became enraged and despondent when Alan overslept on day four of his classes. Alan's father yelled at him, urging him to wake up and labeling him a "lazy kid." The insults escalated as his father unfavorably compared him to other kids. "All you have to do is minimal work, and they're working their butts off doing full-time jobs!" The verbal barrage not only continued throughout the day, but highlighted the perceived inadequacy with which his father viewed Alan and demeaned Alan's work ethic. Alan expressed sadness and frustration that his parents could not give him credit for his effort; they simply could not understand that his neurocognitive challenges were very difficult for him. He further explained that when he puts in the work, he is also vulnerable to failure, and that rejection feels deeply wounding and very scary to him. Through working together, Alan's parents developed a greater understanding and were ultimately receptive to Alan's feelings. Gratefully they also expressed remorse that they had underestimated his difficulties.

## UNDERSTANDING THE FIGHT, FLIGHT, OR FREEZE RESPONSE

Walter Cannon first described the fight, flight, or freeze response to trauma, which is now widely popularized as a way of understanding and treating anxiety and stress.[1] We can see this response in animals who "play dead" in response to an aggressive animal. Our nervous system is designed to have automatic responses to stress. We either go out to slay the woolly mammoth, stay inside our cave until the threat passes, or shut down in response to panic. Children with neurodivergent learning styles experience an overwhelming amount of stress in school. Their responses can be aggressive ("I hate math"), avoidant ("I can't do this"), or complete disengagement (falling asleep in class). Each response illustrates the tremendous stress that school produces in children with neurocognitive disorders. In order to counter the destructive impact of this stress, it is essential that teachers and parents understand this cycle and intervene to reduce it. Sometimes simply offering a pat on the back, removing a student from the task, and giving them concrete strategies are enough to break the cycle and move students toward productivity.

## SELF-ESTEEM

For children with attention deficit disorder, the ability to create and sustain a coherent self-image is hampered by the erratic and inconsistent quality of their work, relationships, and regulation of feelings. They cannot rely on themselves to fully deliver on their goals, so they end up in an untenable situation, either enduring the frustration and disappointment that comes from not being able to produce or withdrawing from the task by procrastinating and coming up with maladaptive strategies—such as lying, cheating, and submitting assignments at the last minute—to get their work done. Sometimes, as the adrenaline kicks in and they are finally able to focus, they can complete their work as the deadline approaches. Nonetheless, their work is still done in haste and often falls short of the requirements. This disastrous cycle can continue for many years and leads to significant dysfunction, particularly as children mature and need to expand their academic and professional goals. Again, it is essential to understand that the neurodivergent child is not a sociopathic liar but rather simply and straightforwardly overwhelmed by the academic demands and neurologically incapable of meeting expectations.

Adam, an extremely articulate and socially mature seventeen-year-old boy, was locked in a toxic cycle with his mother regarding his schoolwork. When asked about homework assignments, he invariably lied to his mother. When his mother then discovered that he had not handed in his assignments, she would become intensely frustrated, yell, and feel dismayed. Adam wanted to please his mother, but he could not complete his work. Testing revealed that Adam suffered from severe ADD. Once I recommended academic support and medication, Adam was able to complete his work and the conflicts with his mother abated.

## SELF-ADVOCACY

Helping your child advocate for him- or herself is a crucial step in empowering them to become active and effective learners and members of the community. As a parent, you can facilitate self-advocacy by explaining to your child how his or her learning difference works and what steps to take to compensate for their challenges. You can brainstorm with him or her about which strategies will work at home and in school. You can encourage your child to communicate with family members, teachers, and peers regarding the nature of his or her deficits and what specific accommodations he or she requires.

For children with ADD, here are some specific strategies and ways to introduce them to their learning issues. A good first step is to acknowledge and explain that they tend to have difficulty focusing, paying attention, and listening. I find the use of analogies helpful. For example, a comparison between attention and a flashlight with several settings seems to make a lot of sense to my students. Both can be either intensely on, completely off, or erratically blinking. I then introduce several techniques to improve focus. For example, we can use the Pomodoro method, which consists of studying in timed intervals. Its inventor, Cirillo, named it after the timer he used, which was shaped like a tomato (*pomodoro* in Italian). He found that breaking a large task into smaller, manageable, timed units is the most effective way to study. He recommended a timer for a thirty-minute cycle: twenty-five minutes of work time and a five-minute break. For children, I may adapt it to ten or fifteen minutes of work time, depending on the nature of the task and the child's attention span. In class, I encourage students to take a daydreaming break or walk around the classroom in order to give the "attention muscles" a break and rejuvenate. I explain that breaks must be short, and you can't do anything compelling such as video games on your break. It is just to give yourself a rest. In school, I ask the teacher to be mindful of these children's needs and provide opportunities for them to stretch their legs and leave the classroom. For example, giving a student a job such as handing out papers or going on an errand would be very helpful. These techniques greatly facilitate a child's ability to focus when in the classroom and improve confidence and self-esteem, as everybody likes to feel productive.

Children with ADD as well as children with language-based learning disabilities often have trouble with multiple directions or processing complex verbal information. Parents or teachers can encourage them to write down directions or provide directions in written form for them. I also encourage students to clarify the directions before they start the task by asking adults to repeat the directions or asking friends about the task to clarify the expectations. Explaining to students that they may miss key words and then get confused can help them understand the need for clarification. Similarly, encouraging these students to raise their hands when they are confused is essential to compensate for their difficulty with processing information and also to cultivate self-advocacy. Children with dyslexia can benefit from help from a peer or teacher if there are specific words that they are unsure of. They can also use technology aids such as audible books and programs that read aloud to you to improve reading comprehension. Children with dyscalculia can use adapted calculators, watch videos explaining math concepts, and use manipulatives such as blocks and tiles to solve problems and understand concepts.

Here's an anecdote illustrating the usefulness of helping children advocate for themselves. After I diagnosed a seven-year-old boy with dyslexia, he created a signup sheet for his classmates to take turns helping him if he didn't understand what he was reading. He explained to them, "I have dyslexia and need help with reading some words." He then confidently read a word problem aloud and solved the answer. With a smile, he joyfully announced, "I didn't need any help with this one!"

## WHEN A CHILD RESISTS HELP

Some children are intensely embarrassed by their challenges and go to great lengths to avoid being singled out. As one vivacious girl with dyslexia commented, "I feel like I am in a fishbowl with teachers staring at me and offering me help." Other children poignantly lament being pulled out of class, taking a test in a different location, and feeling overwhelmed by the level of support. Empathizing with a child's intense feelings is critical to help alleviate their anxiety and feelings of discomfort. Removing the stigma and shame associated with the diagnosis and the need for help can be accomplished by referencing successful figures who have had similar challenges as well as discussing friends and family members who also required extra help and support. Again, never miss an opportunity to highlight your child's areas of strength and their triumphs.

## MANAGING EXPECTATIONS

When children first come in for testing, parents and teachers are often confused about what expectations are reasonable for these children. Often there is a significant mismatch between expectations and performance, leading to a cycle of disappointment, frustration, hurt, and avoidance. An example of a bright, verbal eight-year-old boy with significant ADHD illustrates this principle.

Billy's father explained that dinnertime was a battle because Billy could not sit at the table. His father frequently remarked to him, "Why can't you sit at the table? Please sit down and finish eating. You can't get up until you have finished your plate." But Billy continually got up, ran around the table, out of the room, and never finished eating. Most evenings, Billy cried at least once during dinner and seemed bewildered by his father's expectations. I explained that Billy could sit for only approximately five minutes. Billy's father then asked me if it would be okay if Billy brought a book to the table because then he would sit still and eat. The parents implemented book time at dinner, and all conflict and tears stopped.

## WHAT ABOUT NONVERBAL LEARNING DISORDERS?

Understanding that children with nonverbal learning disorders (NVLD) have real trouble with paper management and accomplishing visual-spatial tasks is the first step to helping them use strategies that facilitate task completion. Keeping track of appointments and assignments in a planner is essential to help them stay organized. Encouraging them to take a picture of the board is useful to get a real-life picture of their homework assignments. When children understand that they cannot remember their assignments unless they write them down in multiple places, they become very creative. For example, one very motivated teenager put twenty Post-it notes on her wall with all her assignments. When she completed a task, she removed the Post-it from the wall. Having concrete visual aids such as these—as well as planners, calendars, and a whiteboard—is so helpful to organizing.

## AUTISM SPECTRUM DISORDER

How can you help your child with autism spectrum disorder (ASD) negotiate the demands of school and home life? Preparing for transitions is one essential step to facilitate a smooth entrance into school. Giving your child sufficient time to prepare—to get dressed, eat breakfast, and so forth—can make a big difference in the mornings. People with ASD often get overstimulated, so building in sensory breaks is critical. For example, they often need an hour or two when they come home to unwind. Helping them identify relaxing activities and encouraging them to take time for themselves can be the critical ingredient for the successful completion of homework.

## SOCIAL CUES

As discussed earlier, social skills are a huge part of your child's life. You can help him or her better understand social situations and become more adept with negotiating friendships, which will improve emotional well-being. First, it is paramount that parents and teachers are aware of and involved with the child's social skills. Nobody is born knowing how to make friends, and children with neurocognitive challenges often require extra instruction and support in this area, just as they do academically. Being present and arranging social opportunities for your child can greatly facilitate friendships and skills. Organizing the right type of social situation also leads to success. I usually recommend a low-key, structured activity such as bowling or a board game to help break the ice, provide a medium level of stimulation, and appeal to children with diverse levels of skill. Going to a movie is another excellent way to socialize, because you can then discuss the movie after seeing it. In general, watching a movie or TV show with your child can be an excellent platform to discuss the interpersonal nuances presented in the show.

As a parent or teacher, you wear many hats, particularly when working with children with neurocognitive challenges; being a social coach is one of the many jobs that you are asked to juggle. For children with ADD, reminding them not to interrupt, to focus on the conversation, and to track the topics can be very helpful. For children with NVLD, helping them understand facial expressions, body language, and spatial cues is key to their success. For children with ASD, helping them acquire empathy and develop eye contact is essential.

To sum up all that we have covered in this chapter, understanding the complex nature of your child's challenges can help you to be his or her best advocate! As parents and teachers, we can brainstorm, cheerlead, nudge, and praise our children to help them flourish both academically and socially.

CHAPTER SIX

# ACCOMMODATIONS AND MODIFICATIONS IN SCHOOL AND AT HOME

Children with neurocognitive issues typically need accommodations and modifications both in school and at home to help them succeed academically, socially, and emotionally. Accommodations generally involve changes in the learning environment or in the way that tasks are presented in order to make it easy for children to participate and learn. These changes can include additional time for assignments, seating arrangements, or the use of assistive technology. Modifications involve altering the curriculum to meet the particular needs of a student. This could mean adjusting the content level of difficulty, such as reducing the number of homework problems on a math sheet to ensure a more inclusive learning experience. Both accommodations and modifications are tailored to address specific challenges that children with neurocognitive issues face, fostering an environment where they can thrive and reach their full potential.

Your job, as either a parent or a teacher, is to get your child all the help he or she needs. Fortunately, we have the law on our side! Starting in the late 1960s and early 1970s, brave and savvy parents and advocates for children with learning disabilities sued the educational system to guarantee that children with neurocognitive challenges receive an "equal" education opportunity. It took decades of stressful litigation but ultimately the federal government ruled that children with disabilities were entitled to a free and public education. The Education for All Handicapped Children Act of 1975 (EAHCA) provided funding to states to assist them in educating students. A cornerstone of this legislation was the Individuals with Disabilities Education Act of 1997, which provided funding for each state, with the goal of providing full educational opportunities for students with disabilities.[1]

The benefit of this groundbreaking legislation is that all public schools are mandated to evaluate children who may have disabilities. Children with identified disabilities receive an Individualized Education Plan (IEP) that outlines the test results, identifies reasonable goals for the student, and mandates accommodation and intervention. If a child does not need an IEP, he or she can also receive a 504, which is a one-page document with a diagnosis and recommendations. Accommodations are considered "reasonable and appropriate" to the extent that they remove disability-related barriers so that students with disabilities are afforded the same access to learning and opportunity to demonstrate knowledge and skills as nondisabled peers.[2]

Despite legislation and our understanding that children need these accommodations, educators still struggle to create policies that are perceived as both "fair" and devoid of unwarranted advantages. Parents and teachers need to be armed with facts and empowered to advocate for their children, making certain that children with needs receive appropriate accommodations and interventions. One such parent is Elaine, the mother of my patient Tommy, an exceptionally intelligent and academically accomplished fifteen-year-old boy who was referred for testing because he had been running out of time on tests and receiving Bs instead of his usual As. Testing indicated that he was a brilliant student with exceptionally low reading speed (7th percentile). As a result, he was extremely stressed, could not complete tests, and was anxious about his grades. Elaine leapt into action, leveraging my report to advocate for Tommy at school. Her efforts convinced the school to grant him extended time in order to complete his work. Tommy not only caught up, but excelled in his studies, dramatically improving his mood.

Another essential skill for parents and teachers involves negotiating the Byzantine world of the board of education in order to ensure their students receive appropriate accommodations. The board of education is a complex system with many, often frustrating, procedural requirements to which families must adhere in order to get their children appropriate intervention. For example, for a child who requires a comprehensive assessment, their family must be interviewed for a social history, and an

IEP meeting is convened to review the results and determine the need for services, which may be denied. Even so, parents at this juncture still have the option to appeal and proceed to an impartial hearing. Your student's psychologist/evaluator is a valuable source of information and can serve as a guide in this epic effort to help negotiate the nuts and bolts of the process. I have shepherded many families in their quest to help their children obtain services. The experience of my patient Ryan's family is an example of the many steps needed to ensure appropriate school placement.

When I assessed Ryan, a painfully shy and withdrawn thir-teen-year-old boy, testing revealed a debilitating depression that re-quired a special school to provide therapy and behavioral support in class. In his mainstream school, he was not able to participate or engage with the material. He spent most of the day with his head on the desk and a blank expression on his face. Clearly, he was inappropriately placed in a mainstream public school. His mother, Julia, was initially resistant to my suggestion of special education placement and was apprehensive about the recommendation. I encouraged her to tour the school and explained its benefits for Ryan. After Julia toured the program, she was extremely enthused about enrolling Ryan. In fact, she enrolled him right away! Then came the next step: getting funding. I explained the process to Julia, and she got the ball rolling. Ryan, Julia, and I were all present at the board of education's IEP meeting for Ryan. Julia had provided them with my report recommending a special education placement, which I also presented at the meeting. While there, Ryan attested to the benefits of his new school program. Ryan's teachers reported that he was coop-erative and responsive in class, although he demonstrated fatigue and low stamina. I also stressed the impact of Ryan's challenges and need for a special education program. Gratefully and appropriately, the board of education granted Ryan the funding he deserved.

## ACCOMMODATIONS

Let's begin by going over typical accommodations that you can reason-ably expect your school to provide for your child with neurocognitive challenges.

## Tests

Extended time on tests and assignments is a very common accommodation, which levels the playing field by helping children compensate for slower processing speed. Even if children are able to complete tests on time, they are often under pressure, rush through the material, and do not have time to double-check their work. This is a commonly requested accommodation because both attention and learning difficulties contribute to slowed speed. Some children are beyond thrilled to have this accommodation and acknowledge that it makes a world of difference in their ability to perform on tests and get good grades. Other children are very embarrassed to accept the extra time; they worry that their peers will be judgmental, thinking they are "stupid" because they read or write slowly. We need to reassure those students that they are just as smart and capable as their peers and that getting extra time is not a reflection of their intelligence. Likewise, parents have their own issues with extended time; they believe that the accommodation doesn't reflect life in the "real world." Further, they think that we are not preparing children adequately for a future and career in which they will be expected to perform at the same rate as their peers. To parents with such concerns, I explain that although there will be many instances when their student may not need the extra time, we have to secure them this accommodation for when they do need it. Another helpful accommodation to recommend is testing in a quiet, separate location that improves focus and reduces anxiety. Similarly, if necessary, we can recommend that the teacher read directions aloud to the student, ensuring that he or she understands the instructions. Last, we can recommend frequent breaks during testing so that the student can move around, stretch, and relax. I cannot articulate more strongly how beneficial all of these accommodations can be when students take tests.

An additional accommodation for tests is to allow students to mark responses in a booklet rather than a Scantron, the response sheet that requires filling in bubbles corresponding to the answers. Many students with learning disorders (LD) and attention deficit disorder (ADD) find the Scantron confusing and visually overwhelming. They may be at risk of skipping lines, leading to errors that impact their overall test performance. Completing the items in a booklet is much easier and also improves speed and accuracy. These accommodations appear trivial, but they can make a world of difference to students with ADD, LD, or autism spectrum disorder (ASD). By adapting the format to better suit the needs of students, educators can create a more inclusive testing environment, allowing these students to demonstrate their understanding and knowledge effectively.

Randy, an outgoing and athletic fourteen-year-old boy, breezed through junior high school when enrolled in a school that emphasized projects and hands-on learning but was overwhelmed with both the homework load and timed tests at his new, more traditional high school. He reported that he ran out of time on tests, leaving questions unanswered, and lacked time to double-check his work. As a result, his bubbly demeanor was replaced by worry and fear; he became permanently sleep deprived because he stayed up late at night to finish his work. Testing revealed that he was a bright, academically capable student with extremely slow reading speed. With accommodations for extra time, Randy learned techniques to improve his speed, his life changed, and he returned to his usual happy self.

## Classroom

Classroom accommodations enable modifications in the learning environment to create a friendlier and more comfortable space for students with disabilities, helping them compensate for their learning challenges. For example, children with ADD and auditory processing difficulties greatly benefit from sitting in front of the class and getting special attention from the teacher. A gentle tap on the shoulder, a reminder to focus, and pointing to the correct line can help students attend and engage. Children with auditory processing challenges can be provided with a headset so the teacher's voice is piped directly into their ears; improved acoustics in the classroom can also make all the difference, as it allows them to understand classroom instruction. Movement breaks are another frequently recommended accommodation, especially for children with ADD. I often advise children to leave their classroom and engage in short bursts of physical activity, such as jumping jacks or running. In this way, they let off steam, coming back to the classroom refreshed and better able to focus.

My patient James, an athletic, engaging eighth grader, ran into significant problems at school because he was so jumpy, fidgety, and impulsive. He often interrupted his teachers, distracted his peers by chatting with them, and blurted out both appropriate and inappropriate comments. His evaluation revealed attention deficit hyperactivity disorder (ADHD), and I recommended giving him frequent "action" breaks. James loved this accommodation and immediately began taking advantage of the recommendation to leave the classroom, run up the stairs, and return to class restored, refreshed, and able to refocus. His parents happily reported that his teachers unanimously described a more relaxed, less distracted student.

### Previewing and Access to Notes

Another very effective suggestion is to allow students to preview classroom material. This can be accomplished in a variety of different ways. For example, watching a movie version before reading the required book, parents taking their student to a museum to get context for a history or science topic, or a special education teacher pre-teaching concepts ahead of classroom instruction. Previewing is a wonderful technique, giving students the information they need ahead of time so they can fully understand the topic in class. In this way, children with neurocognitive issues are given an opportunity to excel and feel confident. I also help students come up with questions or comments that they can generate in class to further cultivate confidence and participation.

My patient Matt, a highly anxious ninth grader with dyslexia, was having difficulty reading the required book for his class. Working together, we began discussing the concepts of the book and relating them to his experience. We discussed the main characters, utilizing a visual outline to deepen his understanding of them. With this strong foundation, only then did we dive into the book. After we took turns reading—first me to him, then him to himself—we discussed what we had read. We came up with questions he could ask and comments he could contribute about the book in class. These techniques helped tremendously; Matt relaxed, enjoyed the book, and ultimately participated in class.

As discussed earlier in this book, listening and writing at the same time can be enormously taxing. Therefore, giving students with ADD and LD access to class notes can be enormously helpful: they don't have to listen and write in class at the same time, and, because they can read the notes after class, they do not need to worry about missing information. This can significantly enhance their overall understanding, concentration, and class participation, ensuring that they perform their best on assessments and tests.

## Language Waiver

Children with ADD and LD often find learning a foreign language exceedingly difficult, as it relies on memory, facility with words, and ability to shift between languages. A foreign language waiver in which the student is exempt from taking a foreign language is actually one of the most common accommodations for students with learning challenges. Students can often receive academic support in place of the language class or use that time to do their homework. Taking American Sign Language is another excellent alternative to a foreign language requirement.

## Writing

Use of a laptop is commonly recommended for students with learning issues, although today most students use laptops, with or without neurocognitive challenges. There are special computer programs geared to students with ADD, LD, and ASD, which should be encouraged. First, using Audible or any program that reads text aloud is incredibly helpful for students with reading difficulties as well as those with ADD. Second, speech-to-text programs can be a lifesaver to help students get their ideas on paper and organize their thoughts. Third, using common writing aids such as spell-check and Grammarly can markedly improve spelling and syntax. Last, special writing programs such as Inspiration create an outline for students and streamlines the writing process. Of note, there is now increased interest and enthusiasm for using artificial intelligence (AI) programs, such as ChatGPT, which can transform the writing experience for students. Obviously, students require coaching and assistance on how to use AI properly. For example, AI can help students organize their thoughts or come up with a good topic sentence but should not be used to write the entire paper for them.

My patient Sally, a sixteen-year-old girl with dyslexia, was able to completely transform her writing experience by using speech-to-text technology. Prior, writing was a laborious and frustrating process. Sally would "dumb down" her ideas and use poor word choices, as she was not comfortable expressing herself on paper. She was worried about spelling errors and explained that her mind shut down when she was writing. Sally required a great deal of help at every step of the process, from writing to proofreading to editing. But today, Sally works independently, dictating anything written, including emails, texts, papers, and outlines. This frees her up to use her extensive vocabulary and sophisticated ideas.

### Reading

Teachers and parents can provide a variety of tools to help children with reading difficulties excel in the classroom. Before diving into a book, teachers can provide students with a thumbnail sketch of the main characters, a plot summary, and important vocabulary. This information facilitates reading comprehension and speed. In addition, graphic organizers, such as markers and sticky notes, are excellent devices to help children organize the words on the page in a way that makes sense to them. Some readers do better with large-print options; others enjoy listening to the audio version of a book while following along visually. Last, the use of mnemonic devices (memory techniques) can facilitate retention in students with poor working memory. For example, an acronym such as "Roy G. Biv" can be used to help students remember the colors of the rainbow.

### Math

When children have difficulty with math, I often recommend the use of a calculator both to increase speed and to improve accuracy of computation. A general principle for helping students who struggle with math is to make sure the problems are clearly written, well organized, and provide plenty of space for them to do their work. Extra-large graph paper is an amazing tool to improve accuracy when solving math problems. Students can also highlight the arithmetic signs, such as addition and subtraction, so they do not get confused or make careless errors. Finally, teachers can help students circle key words in word problems so they can better understand the directions.

Patricia, a bubbly nine-year-old girl, expressed that she was "bad" at math and despondent when faced with math problems. Her tutor broke down the problems in small steps, painstakingly reviewing each with her. This method is called "scaffolding" and can be used in all subjects to help students with neurocognitive challenges master material. In addition, Patricia's tutor gave her extra-large graph paper and taught her to highlight the mathematical symbols, so she did not get confused about which operation to perform. After a few months, Patricia confidently approached her teacher with a smile on her face and asked her for a math worksheet.

## Accommodations for Students with Language-Based LD

What do students with language-based LD need to succeed in the classroom? Since children with this challenge lack facility with words, an emphasis on using visual materials can greatly help them understand what they are learning. Visual aids include graphic organizers such as sticky notes, "cheat" sheets, and highlighters. Using "hands-on" materials, such as cubes and tiles, can also help the students better understand math concepts. Additionally, giving children notes or outlines before the lecture can help with following class discussions and retaining information. Asking students to repeat or write down important words or concepts similarly helps with remembering lectures. As noted earlier, previewing the material is always a fabulous technique: the teacher can provide students with key words or key concepts ahead of time, so they come into the class armed with information that helps them participate and engage with the material. Last, for older students, recording the lecture can be incredibly helpful, because they can listen to it again and again, referring back to key moments to fully grasp the information presented.

## Scheduling Flexibility

Many students with neurocognitive challenges demonstrate slowed speed that causes them a lot of anxiety both in the classroom and at home. They underperform because they cannot complete tests in time or double-check their work and often get overwhelmed by the homework load. Teachers can offer these students more time to complete assignments, shorter work periods and assignments that cover the same work, as well as more frequent breaks. Extended time can be a game changer, as students have the opportunity to showcase their best work without being penalized for their slowed processing speed. Sarah's story is a common one. A bright, verbal tenth grader who consistently received lower grades on her math tests and assignments because she failed to complete them on time, Sarah simply avoided assignments because they took so much time; she would then stay up late into the night to complete her work. When given the opportunity to finish fewer problems and receive extra time on tests, her grades dramatically improved, her sleep habits returned to normal, and she began enjoying doing homework.

### Accommodations at Home

Your child with neurocognitive challenges requires accommodations at home as well as in the classroom. Understanding how their challenges impact their ability to listen to directions, do chores, do their homework, and get along with you is essential to creating a plan that will help them succeed. Slowed speed is a genuine problem at home as your child often lags behind in every area: taking longer to leave the house, clean up his or her room, come to the dinner table, and get ready for bed. Breaking down the task into components and helping your child with whichever task is at hand is an accommodation that can be remarkably helpful. For example, if you want your child to clean his or her room, give one simple instruction such as, "Please take all dirty clothes from the floor and put them in a hamper." The directness of this simple request is far more effective than a blanket request to "clean the room" because children with neurocognitive issues often don't know where or how to start.

Homework is another potential area of conflict. Providing the hands-on support they need helps children compensate for their difficulties. I know parents worry about children becoming "dependent," and although it is important to encourage them to be independent, the most important principle is to help them succeed and remove the support gradually. Think about learning to ride a bicycle. We use training wheels with the understanding that, with proficiency, we ultimately remove them when our children are ready. Homework helpers and executive functioning coaches are also good resources for children to improve academic and organization skills. Using a whiteboard or a planner gives you and your child visual reminders of what needs to be done. I often recommend a checklist of tasks that need to be completed every morning and every night. This helps your child understand what he or she needs to do without you nagging them, a bottleneck that unnecessarily harms relationships.

## MODIFICATIONS

Modifications can significantly change curriculum as well as grading criteria. The idea is to align demands and capabilities. This is in contrast to accommodations, in which there are alterations in the *method* of delivery (for example, extended time), but the student is still given the same material and graded like everybody else. Modifications ensure that your child is graded relative to his or her abilities. Here are some types of modifications for textbooks, curriculum, the classroom environment, and assignments that have been very helpful for students with disabilities.

### Special Education

This refers to placement in a small, structured setting that gives your child the opportunity to learn in a small class size with specialized instruction. This can manifest in various forms, depending on the evaluation and school recommendations. A child may be placed in a special education class with opportunities to mainstream in nonacademic subjects such as recess and lunch; a child can attend some special education and some mainstream classes depending on their level of competence; or they can attend a private special education school where all the classes are special education only. Many students with neurocognitive challenges require these placements, and they are essential for success. Discovering a place where your students will thrive and learn how to compensate for their disabilities can be a full-time job. I highly recommend networking with other parents and professionals who can provide support and information.

## Curriculum

Children with neurocognitive challenges can benefit from being asked to complete shorter assignments. In addition, coming up with alternate assessments or tasks to written work such as projects, posters, and oral tests can greatly facilitate improved performance.

## Grading

Changes in grading standards are a common form of modifications. When students with neurocognitive challenges have difficulty understanding the material, the teacher can give them a partial grade based on their effort. If a student does poorly on tests but is able to engage with the material and participate in class, showing their mastery of the material in other ways, such as projects and verbal participation, the teacher can give those activities more weight than the test grades. A wonderful technique is allowing children to revise their work on the tests, giving them a grade for their corrected work. This technique helps those students with poor recall to show their true knowledge and grasp of concepts. Using a pass/fail system for struggling students can also allow students to get credit for their work and endure the humiliation of a poor grade.

Sally, our high school student with dyslexia, was exceptionally diligent and motivated but she struggled on test performance due to her poor memory. Although she studied and was able to explain the concepts, she often missed details due to her poor working memory. She took full advantage of the option to revise her tests and then received extremely high grades that accurately reflected her level of effort and grasp of the material.

## NEUROCOGNITIVE ASSISTIVE TECHNIQUES

Congratulations! Your child now has accommodations and modifications! They, and you, will be very relieved. We see how helpful these are for our kids. What else can we do to help them thrive in the classroom, at home, and socially?

Neurocognitive assistive techniques are methods and strategies specifically designed to help students with neurocognitive challenges compensate for their deficits. In the classroom and at home we can teach specific skills—how to study, how to organize their time and their papers—that will benefit our children academically, socially, and emotionally. We've already covered scaffolding, wherein we give our children support as needed and gradually remove that support once they become proficient. "Chunking" can make a world of difference to our children and is another method of dividing a task into small, manageable pieces and figuring out which cues and prompts are the most helpful. Parents and teachers often intuitively employ these techniques when communicating and working with children with neurocognitive challenges. It helps to be explicit about how you are helping the student and be aware that you are not "babying" them or giving them a "crutch"; rather you are providing them with an effective, research-based strategy for success.

Another successful teaching technique is direct instruction or explicit teaching. This terrific teaching method is amazingly effective, particularly for students with neurocognitive challenges. Each lesson is oriented to a specific goal, giving students opportunities to practice their skills with feedback from the teacher. The lesson is conducted in short, intense spurts, where the teacher makes sure the students are engaged. This differs from ordinary teaching in a number of important ways. First, the pace is slow and steady. The teacher makes sure the students understand the material before he or she moves on. Second, the students practice their skills during the lesson, *not* leaving it for homework as is typically done. Third, each lesson has one goal, and all students need to meet that goal.

For example, in a reading lesson, a teacher might introduce the concept of foreshadowing. The goal would be to have all the students understand and use this concept in a writing sample. The teacher would explain foreshadowing, give some examples from literature that the students have read, and then provide students with a structured writing prompt so they can practice using the technique in the classroom. Importantly, they then get direct, immediate feedback from the teacher. For example, let's say students are reading *The Giver*, a novel about a dystopian world. The teacher would pick a passage that foreshadows important information about the main character and ask students to highlight the sentences that foreshadow these traits and discuss why they might be important. She would then ask the class to write a paragraph about a main character that uses foreshadowing. This example shows how a thoughtful and comprehensive approach can truly help students.

## METACOGNITIVE INTERVENTIONS

Metacognitive interventions are terrific for helping students to become better learners by teaching them to think about how they learn. Metacognition is the ability to observe one's own learning process. This is important for these students, as they often need to modify instruction and adapt to their deficits. We can teach your child specific strategies including rehearsal (repeating new information), elaboration (summarizing, paraphrasing), and organization, such as note-taking methods. A critical and meaningful skill that I teach is estimating task difficulty and strategizing how to pace themselves accordingly.

Alan, an articulate twelfth grader with ADD, was having difficulty completing long-term assignments. I suggested we come up with a plan for how to tackle a research paper by chunking it into small bits, setting goals, estimating the time it would take to complete each unit, and reviewing our plan. As is typical of students with ADD, Alan significantly underestimated the amount of time he needed to complete each goal. I suggested he triple his time estimate, which helped him figure out how much time he needed to allot for each page. We worked on the paper together and then we set small, manageable goals for him to complete independently. For example, we came up with a research question, and his goal was to identify three sources of information. We then read the sources together, took notes, and used the notes to create an outline. Alan's goal was to elaborate on the very detailed outline that we created together. With these techniques, Alan was able to hand in his research paper on time and received an excellent grade. Equally important is that he felt in control of his work and was learning the skills he needed to function independently.

## MOVING FROM CONCRETE TO ABSTRACT

Students with neurocognitive challenges often struggle with thinking and articulating abstractly. For example, when Sally tries to explain a scientific concept, such as the water cycle, she might get confused about the steps and not understand the main idea—that water is cycled through various stages and states. Therefore, an important teaching technique involves moving from the concrete to the abstract, thus helping each student develop a solid mastery of abstract concepts. Here is an illustrative example.

Leslie, a student with nonverbal learning disorder (NVLD), was taught problem-solving skills to improve her understanding of and performance in math. Her tutor began explaining the concept of multiplication using blocks, then the tutor progressed to visual images (designs), and then ultimately to solving the problem using numbers. This sequential method was very exciting for Leslie, as she was able to understand the concepts before being asked to memorize the facts. Her tutor explained that it was important for her to be able to grasp the underlying concepts, as she was very bright and comprehended ideas but had difficulty with memorization. Leslie was able to internalize these insights and use this type of strategy successfully on her own. Although multiplication facts remained difficult for her, she figured out a strategy that worked for her, enabling her to successfully solve math problems on her own.

## ASSISTIVE TECHNIQUES FOR SPECIFIC DISORDERS

For students with learning disorders, there are specialized techniques designed to assist with specific challenges. These techniques cater to the unique aspects of each disorder, providing targeted support for their individual needs. Tailored strategies can empower children to thrive academically and build confidence in their education.

### Attentional Difficulties

What do kids with ADD need to succeed in the classroom? The buzzword is "executive functioning skills." But what does that mean? Kids with ADD need a secretary, someone who organizes their assignments, manages their calendars, and takes care of the logistics and paperwork! Happily, we can teach them these skills and help them become their own secretary, which both boosts self-confidence and is less expensive! Executive functioning coaching helps these students prepare for tests, submit assignments on time, plan ahead so they do not get overwhelmed, and also clean up their backpacks. Helpfully we also introduce the use of a planner as well as technological devices, which help them remember their assignments and complete them on time. A simple planner can be tremendously helpful, as it has sections for each day and other useful features, such as space for a to-do list, areas for long- and short-term assignments, and places to record appointments. There are a million different planners, so be sure to research with your child the planner that appeals the most to him or her. As for ways to use technology for time management and to organize work, children can keep an online calendar, write in the notes section of their phone, and set alarms on the phone.

Leslie, my patient with NVLD and ADD, was diagnosed at an early age. When she came in for treatment, her parents were concerned that she had difficulty submitting homework assignments on time and was extremely "messy" and forgetful. I worked with Leslie to create a plan for her homework and tests. Once we mapped out time estimates, I checked in with her for the actual times that she spent doing the assignment. We discovered that Leslie chronically underestimated the amount of time it took her to do anything, thus resulting in poor time allocation. I also combed through her backpack with her and created a system for filing her papers. Leslie was able to make good use of her planner, which we bought and filled out together, and appreciated not losing papers due to our new filing system. Partnering with patients is a part of my practice that I cherish. Giving my students hands-on strategies and helping them flourish and thrive is incredibly rewarding.

As mentioned earlier, metacognition is the ability to observe your own cognitive process. This is an important skill for students with ADD and LD. These students, in particular, need to become astute self-observers and to come up with ideas about how to learn information, because the traditional methods of instruction often do not work for them. Helping ADD and LD students think of themselves as active learners and giving them ideas about how they can improve their skills is a metacognitive technique that yields amazing results. For example, students might observe that their attention span is fifteen minutes long. We can then help them take a short break every fifteen minutes and then return to task.

What else can we give these kids to help them manage their attention difficulties? As noted, modifications to the environment can include ensuring sufficient space to freely move around, assigning tasks that entail a great deal of movement, and providing a choice of seating that includes bouncy balls or chairs with sensory stimulation. In addition, fidget objects such as stress balls help focus and reduce anxiety.

## Dyslexia

The most effective technique for teaching children with dyslexia is the Orton-Gillingham method. This method consists of phonetic drills that involve review and repetition of phonic rules and skills. For example, your child learns the long *A* sound by reading a list of words that have that sound, such as *bake*, *cake*, and *sail*. Separately, children with dyslexia also benefit from using context clues to understand a story. When teachers or parents explain the context of the story, it helps the student with dyslexia comprehend the material. For example, if the story is set on a desert island, taking time to explain the setting and its implications will help struggling readers better understand the material. Similarly, introducing the main characters and describing them before a child reads the story is another way of using context to facilitate comprehension.

You can also ask children questions to help them figure out the text. For example, "What is the main point of this passage?" Writing the main points down can help children better understand the information; it also helps teachers to accurately determine what your child does or doesn't understand. Similarly, annotating is another useful technique, as students are asked to write notes or summarize the points of the passage.

Modifications to the environment include making use of the numerous technological innovations that support reading and writing for individuals with learning disorders. Phones with speech-to-text conversion, computer programs such as spell-check and Grammarly, and audiobooks are essential tools for school and work.

### Dyscalculia

Students with math disorders benefit from an individualized math program such as the Singapore method, which breaks down the components of the math problems into simple elements. For example, if a child is learning addition, presenting the sequence in both ways is important, as they might not understand that 7 + 3 is the same as 3 + 7. We need to break down these elements to explain to them that these problems are the same. Using manipulatives, such as tiles and blocks to represent numbers, can really help your child better understand how to add, subtract, multiply, and divide. This can help a student move from the concrete to the abstract, ultimately grasping the concepts of numbers and arithmetic.

### Nonverbal Learning Disorder

Children with NVLD have significant difficulty understanding the space around them, thus they often get lost. I recommend clearly marking the classroom and school to aid in moving through the physical space. For example, spaces can be labeled, such as "cubbies," and arrows can be drawn on the floor or walls to indicate different rooms, such as the gym and the cafeteria. In addition, because those with NVLD often have organization difficulties similar to students with ADD, in which both their time and paper management skills are compromised, I recommend using online tools such as calendars, which markedly improve organization and productivity.

### Autism Spectrum Disorder

A big academic and social challenge that children with ASD grapple with is their rigid cognitive style. Because they tend to see situations in a very literal, detail-oriented, and concrete way, they often have a difficult time grasping the gestalt of a situation. In other words, they miss the forest for the trees. We need to teach them how to infer and analyze both social situations and academic tasks. Students with autism spectrum disorder benefit from help in learning how to analyze and respond to inferential questions such as, "How do you think the boy is feeling in the story?" Or "What do you think will happen next?" Scaffolding and direct instruction help these students move beyond the literal interpretation of the text to engage in more nuanced and sophisticated reasoning. For example, when reading a story with these students, you can start by going over the literal meaning of the story and all the details that contribute to the narrative. Once the student has mastered these concepts, you would take it a step further and pose some analytic questions for the student such as, "What is the main idea of this story? How do the characters feel in the story? What do you think will happen next?" These questions help the student use inferential skills. You can also explain how to answer these questions based on the text with a question such as, "The author describes the character as 'scowling' so what feeling is that?"

Children with ASD have great difficulty understanding other people's feelings and motivations. They may seem very unempathic because they are unable to take another person's perspective. Social coaching, using role play, and structured exercises can be very helpful in improving social skills.[3] For example, you and your student may act out a social conflict, discuss the feelings of each character, and learn tools for negotiating conflict.

In one group I ran for boys with autism spectrum disorder, we played a card game requiring them to lie as part of the game. Understanding how to lie successfully incorporates understanding of social nuances. Children with ASD often make insulting comments, since they do not understand what is socially acceptable to say and when to be polite. We often discussed, amid much laughter and boisterous energy, how to catch someone in a lie and how to lie coolly. Of course, lying can be a major social problem, and I, of course, was very clear about what constitutes a polite lie and when it is necessary to tell the truth. The game also taught the boys how to take turns, congratulate each other, and maintain good spirits even if they were losing.

Children with ASD often get easily overloaded by noise and light, so modifications to the environment include dim lighting and soundproofing. Sensory rooms use lights, colors, and textures to provide a calm, serene experience. Weighted blankets and sensory objects such as fidget toys can help quell anxiety and improve focus in those children on the autism spectrum who are easily overwhelmed by sensory stimulation.

## HOW STUDENTS AND PARENTS FEEL
## ABOUT GETTING ACCOMMODATIONS

For students and parents, there are often mixed feelings about receiving accommodations and modifications. For some children and their families, it comes as a relief, and they are often ecstatic about getting the opportunity for their children to finally be able to live up to their potential. Parents often fiercely advocate for their children to get support and are thrilled with the results, particularly when they are rewarded with happier, more productive children! On the other hand, children are often embarrassed about receiving support; they feel singled out and stigmatized by the "special education" label. They lament being pulled out of class, want to be in a mainstream program, or simply desire to fit in with their peers. Sometimes receiving special services can lead to bullying by peers, as children are often allergic to anyone who is "different." Likewise, parents often worry that their children are handicapped, are using such supports as "crutches," and are too dependent on them. Additionally, some parents are ashamed that their child is in special education and feel inferior as a result. Getting support from other families who are in the same boat can go a long way to resolve these feelings of shame and inferiority. Simply recognizing that your child has the capacity to succeed and will flourish in the right environment can be very healing. As parents become more sophisticated, they also become empowered to advocate for their children and often serve as sources of inspiration and support for other families.

As an evaluator and a therapist, I confront this problem head-on with my patients. I reassure my patients and their families that these accommodations are vital and are not "cheating." The student has a real problem and requires real-life intervention in the form of accommodations. Helping them figure out how best to access accommodations is one of the most rewarding parts of my job. For example, I introduce test-taking strategies that allow them to take the best advantage of the extended time. I teach them to read slowly and carefully, highlighting "tricky" words and making sure they don't make careless errors. Once students start using these strategies, they begin performing better on tests, their self-confidence improves, and their level of stress goes way down. The following case illustrates the transformative power of understanding the diagnosis and the need for accommodations.

Paul, an extremely intelligent high school student, was referred for overwhelming anxiety. My testing revealed severe dyslexia as well as depression. An intellectually gifted student with a stellar academic history, he revealed that he had never completed reading any of the books assigned to him in school. He had successfully hidden his challenges in reading from his parents, teachers, and peers. He felt like an imposter and a fraud because he read so slowly. When given some reading help and extended time, his anxiety lifted, and he felt comfortable taking tests for the first time in his life.

## TEACHERS' ROLES

Teachers are on the front lines when it comes to accommodations and modifications in the classroom. Helping teachers understand the need for the accommodations is crucial because they are the key players and partners. Sometimes teachers are skeptical that the student has legitimate neurocognitive challenges. They are also concerned about "fairness" to peers and often are resistant to administering individual test accommodations. In general, they are most receptive to instructional accommodations that can be easily administered to a range of students, such as repeating directions (who doesn't benefit from clarification?) or breaking down the steps of a problem. Sometimes parents and their families meet with frustrating and real resistance. Here's an example illustrating the complexity of getting a school to provide adequate accommodations.

Sally, the bright tenth grader with dyslexia that we met earlier, was mainstreamed from a special education school to a private school that provided a great deal of support. She received extended time, special education instruction, and allowances for spelling. However, at the end of the year, finals were administered as an in-class essay. This type of testing was punitive for Sally; due to her poor working memory and severe dyslexia, she could not construct a coherent, well-organized essay with proper syntax and grammar. Her mother, who proofread her papers, commented that the word choices were often so misspelled you could not figure out their meanings unless she told you what she meant. The examiner asked the school to allow Sally access to notes during the test so she could write out her essays ahead of time, have the chance to make revisions with support, and then write them during the test. The school refused, citing concerns about fairness for the other students. We explained that this testing method was unfair to Sally in light of her learning disorder, and she would not be able to showcase her knowledge of the subject. The school said it would take it under consideration.

## SELF-ADVOCACY

A very important phenomenon in special education is self-advocacy; children need to learn how to self-advocate in order to make good use of resources, to ensure that they get the accommodations they need, and to thrive in the classroom and at home. When your child understands his or her accommodation needs, he or she can successfully communicate them with teachers and peers. Happily, your child can and will improve in confidence and effectiveness as a student.

When Rachel, an articulate twelve-year-old girl, was diagnosed with ADD and dyslexia, I recommended extended time and academic support. Initially, Rachel was reluctant to avail herself of the support and the time. She told me she was worried that her peers and teachers would criticize her. I worked with Rachel to help her understand why she was entitled to the accommodation and how to advocate for herself. I explained that her brain worked differently and that she was a bright, capable student who required the interventions in order to be successful. I reviewed her test scores with her and was able to show that she had significant areas of strength in her analytic abilities but also scored poorly on tests of speed and decoding words. After these interventions, Rachel confidently asserted that she needed both extra time and academic support and was able to arrange meetings with all her teachers to receive her accommodations.

## COMMON MISCONCEPTIONS

What are some common misconceptions that teachers, parents, and students often harbor that make it difficult to maximize the efficacy of accommodations? First, the idea of accommodations as a "crutch" is often mentioned. Parents, teachers, and children are often worried that the support and accommodations are a crutch that they will become somehow dependent on, and it will make their learning challenges worse, not better. At the same time, there is a rigidity in thinking: *there's only one proper way to learn and take tests, and if you deviate from this norm, you are doing it incorrectly and you will not be able to succeed.* Third, there is concern that accommodations are not the "real world," and if we give children accommodations and support, they will fail miserably in college or on the job when they don't get accommodations.

I use the analogy of an "invisible wheelchair" to help people understand the fallacy of these misconceptions. Just as we would not expect wheelchair-bound individuals to walk and would not penalize them for this disability, we cannot expect the individual with neurocognitive impairment to operate as a neurotypical student. When we give accommodations, we are "leveling the playing field"; we are *not* disadvantaging our children with neurocognitive challenges. As they grow, mature, and self-advocate, they will use their unique talents and flourish both despite and because of their challenges.

## HOW CAN ROLE-PLAYING HELP?

Role-playing involves the therapist and patient acting out a scenario to help the patient develop coping strategies and alleviate the anxiety surrounding the situation. Instead of simply discussing the situation and getting insight and advice, the patient literally acts out the scene with facilitation by the therapist. A case example illustrates this technique.

Leslie, the young adult with NVLD mentioned earlier, needed extra time on tests in college but was scared to ask for help from the disability office. We role-played the scenario, with her leaving my office then returning to knock on the door to ask for the accommodation. We also explored her feelings of anxiety and fear of rejection as related to early experiences of bullying and the stigma associated with being taken out of class for services. This exercise allowed Leslie to successfully self-advocate for extended time and gave her the self-confidence to continue to ask for the things she needs.

In sum, receiving accommodations and modifications is an essential ingredient in facilitating academic success. In the next chapter, we focus on the types of therapeutic interventions we can provide for our children with neurocognitive challenges to help them flourish emotionally and socially.

## CHAPTER SEVEN

# TREATMENT OPTIONS FOR CHILDREN WITH NEUROCOGNITIVE CHALLENGES

Unraveling the mystery that your child needs and deserves therapy is an excellent first step, but determining the best approach can also be daunting. What kind of therapy is best for your child? Let's explore some of the treatment options.

Before we begin, it's important to understand what we've discussed in previous chapters: neurocognitive challenges such as learning disabilities, attention deficits, or autism levy a significant emotional and social toll; understandably, your child may feel distressed and frustrated. Receiving academic accommodations, modifications, or support can feel humiliating, infantilizing, and stigmatizing. Experiencing yourself as different from peers and family members may leave a child feeling isolated, inferior, and incompetent. In addition, they may face criticism from peers, teachers, and family members for their academic or social struggles. Most important, repeated experiences of failure are traumatic and can lead to a child's painful feelings of disappointment, frustration, and low self-esteem. So it's really no wonder that many children with learning and attention issues are also diagnosed with anxiety and depression. Thankfully, there are a plethora of wonderful interventions to support your child, reduce anxiety, and improve both their self-esteem and confidence. But how can you best understand what your child needs and which technique would be the most effective?

The first step is to learn about your child's specific profile, which will enable you to choose the most effective intervention. Typically, children with neurocognitive challenges benefit from a multifaceted approach. From my experience, I know how imperative it is to answer a plethora of questions at once, including: What are your child's specific challenges?

How have teachers, peers, and family members responded? What are your child's symptoms? Does your child experience anxiety, depression, low self-esteem, and/or poor social skills? As a partner in your child's care at every level, I intervene to make sure your child is getting academic and, critically, psychological and emotional support. I consult with teachers, tutors, and parents to ensure that everyone is on the same team, supporting your child's best interests. In order to accomplish this, I use a variety of techniques to specifically address anxiety and depression.

Psychoeducation is an important term that I always use when working with children and their parents. What that means is that I intentionally educate everyone in the room about the specific neurocognitive challenge and, most important, how your child is emotionally affected by that disability. It is a game changer when the whole family understands the issues, which include both the specific challenge as well as the concomitant emotional responses to that challenge. Once this happens, family relationships are secured, children start feeling better about themselves, and tensions go way down.

Alan, a morose, sullen seventeen-year-old boy, was always in trouble with his parents because he was on thin ice academically. Tensions escalated into loud, toxic verbal conflicts when Alan's parents erupted every time he neglected his homework or did poorly on a test. Testing revealed Alan had significant attention deficit hyperactivity disorder (ADHD) and anxiety. I recommended medication, therapy, accommodations, and academic support. Alan's father expressed both regret that he berated his son so much and relief that there was help for him. As Alan began to do better in school, his mood improved, and he reported a much better relationship with his parents.

I implement effective strategies to address the daily challenges commonly encountered by children with neurocognitive issues and their families. These include disorganization, poor time management, compromised social interactions, difficulty completing homework, lack of cooperation with household routines and chores, lack of focus, impulsivity, and reduced frustration tolerance among many others. Psychoeducation is a key component, involving a detailed explanation of how these challenges manifest and practical strategies for support. I often recommend techniques, encourage their implementation, and request feedback to tailor a comprehensive plan. This approach works to reduce stress, enhance your child's ability to complete tasks, and compensate for any deficits.

Adam, an energetic, earnest twelve-year-old boy, was referred to me for testing because he was having difficulty completing his homework. The homework battles became so severe that Adam could be found crying most nights, unable to be consoled. When my testing revealed significant expressive writing disorder, I recommended using a speech-to-text technology at home, which alleviated most of Adam's distress regarding homework.

When working in therapy with children, I think of the treatment as having different segments that coordinate with each other. Psychoeducation is the first segment, in which I help your child understand his or her disability, come up with practical strategies, and explore his or her feelings about it. Although psychoeducation is most heavily used at the beginning of treatment, I use it throughout therapy, because your child's feelings about his or her disabilities can arise and change over time depending on the situation.

Lucy, a highly verbal, intelligent seventeen-year-old girl, was diagnosed at a young age with ADHD and autism spectrum disorder (ASD). During our initial work together, I encouraged Lucy to focus on her social skills. We used role-play and emotional support to help her learn how to make friends, something with which she struggled. Happily, Lucy was able to become part of a small group of friends and was socially fulfilled for one of the first times in her life. However, her challenging learning profile and need for support, particularly from her mother, was a source of embarrassment and shame. She voiced that she felt "stupid, like a screwup, and like a fraud" because she required so much help with her papers. I explained to Lucy that getting support was not an indictment of her intelligence or character. She found it immensely helpful when we reviewed her test results, after which she began to better understand her learning profile. Importantly, this allowed her to relax her harsh self-judgments.

Another pivotal role as a therapist working with children with neurocognitive challenges is to consult with the school and family. In order to receive accommodations and support, I need to advocate for your children as well as work with them on understanding and accepting these interventions. Parents need to be educated, as well, to let go of their misconceptions and to support their children both emotionally and academically. Helping all stakeholders and everyone in the system come to terms with the impact of the neurocognitive challenges is a process that takes time and can be deeply emotional for everyone. Shifting from self-blame to acceptance can take years, as these conceptions are part of your child's identity.

James, an avid theater buff and comic-con connoisseur, was diagnosed with attention deficit disorder (ADD) when he was seven years old, from which time he received accommodations and support. He thrived academically and socially but reported disturbingly low self-esteem. He said he was "lazy, procrastinated, and did not make good use of his potential." It took years of painstaking work in therapy for James to understand that he was working really hard and deserved his academic success.

As can be seen from the previous vignettes, children with neurocognitive challenges universally struggle with self-esteem, confidence, and adapting to their areas of deficit. There are also issues that are specific to individual disorders. Let's take a look at them so we can better understand your child's challenges.

## LEARNING DISORDERS

Your child with nonverbal learning disorder (NVLD) is usually highly verbal and articulate. Think of the children who easily chatter, raise their hand often, and are never at a loss for words. However, they are stymied by maps, diagrams, and graphs. They often get lost on their way to or from events, as they have a horrible sense of direction and may not be able to perform tasks that require coordination such as bike riding or tying shoes. Sadly, they are often described as "flighty" or "needy" when they need help with directions or can't perform basic tasks. They also can be quite disorganized and time challenged. They describe themselves as a "mess" and lament how hard it is to organize their room and backpack. Understanding that these problems are due to the wiring in their brains helps them—and you—better accept their challenges, freeing them to problem-solve ways to compensate for their weaknesses.

Leslie, a vivacious fifteen-year-old girl with pink hair, lamented her difficulty with math and directions. She would say to me, "I am so bad at math. I hate it and feel stupid." She further shared, "I am always getting lost going from one class to the other; it is so frustrating!" I banned the word "stupid" from our sessions and focused on explaining to Leslie how her brain works: "You are a left-side brain learner, which is why you are such a wonderful reader and writer, but the right side of your brain doesn't work as well, so you have trouble with visual-spatial tasks such as math." As Leslie began to identify her strengths and see her challenges in perspective, she began to brainstorm strategies to help with her problem areas. She created directional signs and placed them throughout her school, helping her, as well as other students, navigate the premises. Working with a math tutor who helped her understand the problems, she ultimately excelled in her classes. One day she triumphantly exclaimed, "I know I am smart; I just have a NVLD."

Children with language-based learning disorder have the opposite problem. They have such difficulty expressing themselves that they are often tongue-tied in social and academic situations. Because core academic tasks such as reading and writing are significant areas of challenge, their self-esteem suffers, and they frequently describe themselves as "stupid." They can be seen as shy, oppositional, and noncommunicative. Their reticence is misinterpreted as poor behavior, although they very much want to be social and cooperative. It's essential to explain to these children how their language deficits impact them academically and socially. Once they understand the etiology of their issues, they can look for solutions and their self-esteem improves.

Adam, a sweet "self-described nerd," was an avid video game player and tended to be very quiet, as he had expressive language disorder. When talking, he often got frustrated and somewhat strangely exclaimed, "Words!" to express how challenging it was for him to get his words out. I worked with him on understanding why conversation was so stressful for him and helped him with strategies to improve his skills. For example, we brainstormed topics he could discuss with his friends and created questions he could ask his teachers in class. Magically, as Adam improved his ability to use his words, his anxiety disappeared, and he became more engaging and participatory.

## ATTENTION DISORDERS

Your child with ADD also, heartbreakingly, feels "stupid" and "bad." They suffer socially because they blurt out impulsive comments, which are seen as insulting even though they don't mean to be offensive. They have trouble showing up on time for meetings and are labeled as "flaky" and "selfish." They often interrupt their peers and then get reprimanded because they cannot control their behaviors. In school, they can't focus on the work, feel painfully bored, and become known as the "kid who never hands his assignment on time." They feel "weird" and "out of place" because they are so distracted and can't follow the conversation.

Cara, an athletic fifteen-year-old girl, was constantly getting in trouble in school and at home because, according to both her parents and teachers, she "didn't care, had an attitude, lied about handing in her work, never studies, and is always fooling around." Cara reported to me that she was without motivation, that she hated school; she referred to herself as "bored and weird." My testing revealed that Cara had severe ADD and I recommended medication, therapy, and accommodations. I worked with her to help her understand that she did care about doing well and could hand in her work on time, as long as she took her medicine and used her resources. Recently, Cara said, "When I first got diagnosed, I thought the goal was to fix me to be normal. Now I realize that if I learn how to adjust and adapt, I can do really well." I pointed out to her that she is incredibly analytic and intelligent; she thinks out of the box, and I want her to lean *into* the wonderful parts of her brain. She smiled and said something that all therapists want to hear from their patients as they struggle to actualize their potential. She said, "I would never have described myself as analytic or conceptual before but now I see that I am."

## AUTISM SPECTRUM DISORDER

Your child with ASD feels like a fish out of water in social situations. They cannot understand feelings (either their own or other people's) and cannot take another personal point of view. They also don't understand nuances and cues, so often say or do something offensive without meaning to. Their rigidity is extreme; they cannot tolerate even small changes in their routine or their environment. It's easy to see how they can be labeled "rude and defiant." Ariel, a twelve-year-old girl with ASD, was highly anxious about gym class, referred to it as "loud and smelly," and struggled with asking to join games, leading her to spend a significant amount of time on the sidelines. I worked with Ariel on practicing her social skills, an important milestone, and she became capable of initiating game participation.

Now that you understand the significant emotional impact that neurocognitive challenges have on your child, what can *you* do to support him or her? There are many wonderful therapeutic interventions that can be tremendously beneficial. Let's take a look at them with examples to illustrate how they can help.

## PSYCHOEDUCATION

Discussed earlier, psychoeducation is a very valuable technique for you and your child to gain information about his or her diagnosis, to help make good decisions, and to get access to resources. The better informed you are as a parent, the smarter you are about the way you parent your child. The more children understand their learning challenges, the better they can come up with strategies to adapt and adjust. Psychoeducation is used throughout treatment in conjunction with psychotherapy. Here are some psychotherapy interventions that can be used with both you and your child.

## PSYCHOTHERAPY INTERVENTIONS

### Psychodynamic Approach

A psychodynamic approach means that the therapist is interested in exploring your child's feelings and helping them understand their own behaviors. In addition, children with neurocognitive challenges often struggle with intense feelings of shame as they have often experienced repeated failures both academically and socially. These experiences can lead to anxiety, depression, and low self-esteem. In therapy, we can help by understanding and sympathizing with these feelings and helping release this pain. Your child might say that he or she feels like an "imposter" or a "fraud." These feelings are related to shame and deep feelings of inferiority. In my practice, I work with children to understand where these negative self-concepts come from.

Alex, a fourteen-year-old boy with cool glasses and a buzz haircut, proclaimed that he was an "imposter" because he needed so much help to get his work done; sometimes he couldn't get his work done, even with a lot of support! I asked him to have compassion for himself and explained that it takes twice as much energy and commitment for him to do his work than other students, because it was so hard for him to sit and focus. I asked Alex to pretend that he was looking at a friend's work, rather than his own. How would he judge his friend? Over many sessions, Alex began to understand that he did not need to feel shamed by his disabilities.

Psychodynamic therapy is a wonderful intervention for children with ADD because it addresses specific challenges, like impulsivity, a prominent feature of the disorder. The therapist plays a crucial role in assisting children to develop and enhance impulse control, which is an invaluable skill for managing ADD effectively. Children with ADD often run into trouble in social situations, interrupting conversations and blurting out inappropriate comments. Similarly, at school and at home, parents and teachers may become frustrated and angry with these kids because they cannot control their behaviors. Unfortunately, they tend to receive continual negative or accusatory feedback from others, who say cruel things such as, "You're a pest, go away!" or "Why are you not listening to me?" Psychodynamic therapy can help them understand this feedback, accept their challenges, and learn how to cope with them. Here is an example of how I integrated psychoeducation and psychotherapy to help a worried high schooler do his best.

Joe, a talkative, intellectual sixteen-year-old boy, came to see me to better understand his learning style. He shamefacedly related that he often submitted assignments late and would get into trouble with his parents and teachers. Joe, an exuberant and loud boy, had trouble sitting still in class. He frequently made jokes and enjoyed both the attention from his peers and the distraction it provided from his studies. Needless to say, his parents and teachers were very worried about him. In fact, Joe was also very worried about himself. He was frustrated that he tended to procrastinate and knew that he was skating on thin ice in class. When I first began to treat him in therapy, we established that testing revealed that his behaviors were the result of ADD and could be remedied with medicine and tutoring. In doing so, Joe's grades and homework improved. In therapy, we also discussed how embarrassed he felt when he got in trouble and how small he felt in comparison to his siblings. Joe so much wanted his parents and teachers to be proud of him. As we explored these feelings of shame, he began to feel more confident and less worried. He was thrilled with his improved grades and felt better about himself.

Joe's story shows how incredibly destructive feelings of shame can be. When you are embarrassed, you just want to disappear. No wonder it is so hard for children who are ashamed about their skills to do their work. This sets in motion a vicious cycle: the more they avoid their work, the more parents and teachers are frustrated with them. In therapy, we can help your child dispel the shame related to academic tasks. As their confidence improves, they begin to be able to tackle their responsibilities more effectively, which in turn lets them experience praise for their efforts. This validation empowers them to keep trying and working.

### Learning Disorders and Psychodynamic Therapy

Children with learning disorders greatly benefit from psychodynamic therapy to help improve their confidence, alleviate anxiety regarding their skills, and shore up their self-esteem. Having a learning disorder can be very isolating, because children can feel so alone in thinking that no one else can understand them. In therapy, we can help them communicate their needs to their family and teachers, allowing them to feel more supported. As children with learning disorders experience repeated failures, it is crucially important to help them understand their areas of strength and encourage them to pursue activities in which they excel. Ann, a highly anxious, introverted twelve-year-old girl with NVLD, came to see me because she was friendless. She shared that she had been bullied at school and excluded from social activities. She felt that the social ostracism was related to the many services she received in school due to her learning disorder. At her new school, I encouraged Ann to join the theater club, since she was interested in drama. I explained to her that she was highly verbal and articulate and that peers would respect her knowledge. She hesitantly joined the drama club but before long had a close-knit group of friends whom she enjoyed hanging out with.

## Autism Spectrum Disorder and Psychodynamic Therapy

Children with ASD often want therapy because they feel depressed or anxious. They are aware of having trouble fitting in with peers and desperately desire closer relationships. Therapy can address all of these problems. Another significant issue with children with ASD is that they get easily overwhelmed by sensory stimuli such as noise, light, social interactions, and smell. Although at times, they will be unable to verbalize their sensitivity, they feel tremendously agitated and uncomfortable. A good therapist can help children with ASD understand their sensory sensitivities and encourage them to regulate their environment, so they don't get overloaded. Most importantly, the therapist can help children improve their social skills and connect with their feelings.

David, an anxious, self-described nerd, came to therapy because he was feeling a lack of energy and depressed. Although he was very bright and capable, he was having trouble attending school and keeping up with the work. My testing revealed that he had ASD, and we began to work on his symptoms. One of the first suggestions I made was making sure he relaxed at home in a dimly lit room before he started his homework. We also explored hobbies for him that would be rejuvenating. David began playing chess, doing jigsaw puzzles, and collaging as ways to relax. In family sessions, I helped him communicate with his parents and set up a good schedule that was not as stimulating for him. David's mood improved and he was able to attend school regularly.

Psychotherapy is a valuable intervention for children with neurocognitive challenges, but they often require multiple modalities to address their issues. Here are some additional approaches that can help.

## Multimodal Approaches

Cognitive behavioral therapy or CBT is widely used to target symptoms of anxiety. As the name implies, CBT works on our thoughts, feelings, and behaviors. For example, if a child is scared of math, a therapist can help alleviate this fear by slowly introducing mathematical topics, helping them work on math problems in therapy, and giving them homework exercises that involve using math at home. This therapy is often used in addition to psychotherapy and antianxiety medicine when your child has specific anxieties and fears.

Dialectical behavior therapy or DBT is another widely used treatment to help children regulate their behavior. Here, the DBT therapist can provide strategies and tools to help calm patients down and reduce impulsive and aggressive behavior when they feel distressed and anxious. With DBT, children learn to pause before they say or do something, check in with themselves, and better understand when they are feeling frustrated. For example, your child may be taught to use the acronym HALT when they are distressed; this acronym reminds them to determine if they're hungry, angry, lonely, or tired—as these are four at-risk states that can lead to inappropriate behaviors. They learn diverse techniques to encourage thoughtfulness and help them curb impulsivity.

Play therapy for children is a specific form of psychotherapy that uses play to help children express their feelings and better understand their experiences. It's a creative and imaginative technique wherein the child and therapist together create play representation of your child's inner world. Children draw, play board games, play with dolls, and engage in rough-and-tumble play. The relationship with the play therapist is extremely important, as the therapist provides support, validation, and a safe space where children can learn how to express their feelings, solve problems, and gain confidence.

Nancy, a sweet, bubbly five-year-old girl with a short attention span, was referred for play therapy because she was highly anxious about her parents' separation. In therapy with me, Nancy drew pictures and created a weekly story expressing her sadness and confusion. Her stories were populated with monsters, witches, and a little girl who spent her time either running away from these ogres or crying. As we developed the story, I gently introduced alternative scenes for the little girl. Together, we gave her a friend to whom she went when she was feeling sad. We also gave her a magic wand so she could better control the monsters. The power of these creative exercises never ceases to amaze me: Nancy's anxiety lifted, and she was better able to cope with the stress in her family.

What are some key differences between these interventions? CBT and DBT typically involve a limited number of sessions and follow a structured approach using manuals to achieve specific goals, often targeting a particular symptom, such as obsessive behaviors. In contrast, play therapy and psychotherapy offer more flexibility and open-ended timelines. These approaches concentrate on a therapist building a relationship with your child and addressing broader issues, such as self-esteem, social skills, and overall mood. You can choose the intervention that best suits your child based on their symptoms and social/emotional functioning.

### Therapies Specific for Disorders

Cognitive behavior therapy is often used for children with ADHD, as it has been proven to reduce impulsivity and improve focus. Children with ASD benefit from CBT to improve eye contact and engage in conversation. Social skills training using behavioral techniques is an excellent intervention for children who are suffering socially. Psychotherapy is indicated for ADD, learning disorders (LD), and ASD to improve self-esteem and problem-solving skills.

### Group Therapy

Group therapy is a wonderful modality for children because a social environment is most natural. Developmentally, childhood is a time to socialize, and getting along well with peers is a prerequisite for a happy childhood. Group therapy provides a social outlet for children with social challenges. It helps them get along with their peers and learn from them. When children with neurocognitive challenges meet as a group, they can exchange experiences, give each other support, and help with the feelings of isolation and inferiority that so often arise with these disorders.

For many years, I ran groups for children with ADD, LD, and ASD, and I found that the children made remarkable progress with this intervention. With younger children, we played and talked together. Playing gave children the opportunity to learn how to take turns, win and lose gracefully, and cope with feelings of frustration and stress. Conversation was invaluable in helping them learn how to engage and converse with peers and better understand their own challenges. I often introduced activities that helped them focus on their skills. For example, we discussed how to listen empathically and how to gauge whether others are listening to you.

David, a nine-year-old boy with ASD, entered individual and group therapy with me. He was an active participant in group therapy and really enjoyed playing with the other boys, although he tended to blurt out inappropriate comments that were inadvertently offensive. For example, David would comment on someone's body odor or lack of skill in a game. With feedback from me and his peers, he learned to think before he spoke and check in with people. He was able to ask, "Did I insult you?" and became more empathetic and thoughtful.

For children with language-based disorders, language and social skills improve in a group setting, because they are able to practice in a safe environment with accepting peers. I often use the analogy that group therapy is akin to swim practice. You can teach the strokes on dry land but at a certain point, you simply need to get into the water and experience swimming! Group therapy helps children improve their social skills in real life. They banter with the other group members, ask them for advice and support, and negotiate taking turns. For children with nonverbal learning disorders who often have trouble picking up on social cues, they also learn the important skills of recognizing body language and analyzing social situations.

One activity that I used to help children negotiate body space is to practice leaning into someone's space and stating when they felt crowded. The boys loved this activity as it was both funny and fun. Along the way, we discussed how much space to give people and when to recognize when we were being intrusive. We also modeled how to express and interpret feelings by making different facial expressions and then guessing how the person felt. Amid much laughter at the funny faces, the boys gained meaningful insight into facial cues.

As children with ADHD often alienate peers with their impulsivity, interrupting, and poor control over their feelings, a group environment is a perfect setting to learn how to navigate feelings and control these behaviors. It's essential to establish group rules that include no interrupting, being kind and considerate to others, and giving each other respectful feedback. During raucous games and boisterous banter, children with ADD can learn to distinguish between when they are offending their peers or merely having a good time. Helpful statements such as "Look before you leap" prompt them to pause and consider an action before actually acting on it. As the boys empathize and support each other, they feel less alone and gain confidence, a necessary ingredient for success.

## Medication

Medication is often an integral piece of treatment for children with neurocognitive challenges. Medication can be an absolute game changer in helping children with ADD focus or alleviating anxiety in children with ASD. Consultation with a psychiatrist or psychopharmacologist is necessary to ensure that your child receives the appropriate medication. As medication can be a sensitive topic, the therapist can collaborate with the psychiatrist to help the child and family arrive at agreement and make decisions about the type of medicine that would be the most helpful.

## Parent Guidance

Working with your child's therapist is a critically important part of treatment. Parenting a child with neurocognitive issues presents unique challenges, and parents often feel at a loss as to how to best help their child. Having a therapist as a sounding board and ally for this difficult job is both crucial and valuable. Family therapy sessions also can be incredibly helpful to reduce stress and conflict at home. Parents can bring up specific problems they face at home, and the session can focus on brainstorming solutions to address those issues. For example, Claire's parents came to my office for a family session, as they did not know how to help their eleven-year-old daughter with NVLD take daily showers and brush her teeth. They were grateful when we came up with a system that involved writing a daily routine on a whiteboard that Claire would then check off as she completed each task. With reminders and support from me and her parents, Claire began to take daily showers and brush her teeth. Her parents were incredibly relieved that a huge source of daily stress simply disappeared from their lives with this incredibly useful tool. Cutting down on the verbal nagging, it served as a concrete reminder for everyone and also gave Claire the control to complete the activity. It was also a teachable moment, because Claire carried that technique over to her schoolwork and other responsibilities. I always encourage my patients to structure their time and "write it down," creating lists for even the fun activities.

### Modifications of Therapeutic Styles

In addition to integrating multiple therapeutic modalities such as CBT, DBT, and psychotherapy, a therapist often needs to modify the therapeutic approach when working with children with neurocognitive challenges. I find that I need to adjust how I communicate depending on the child's level of comprehension and recall. I am very active with many of my patients, rolling up my sleeves to provide hands-on support rather than just talking about it. Additionally, a collaborative team approach is crucial, as most children with neurocognitive challenges have a team of professionals working with them, including occupational therapists, physical therapists, speech and language therapists, and tutors.

### Therapeutic Styles for Specific Disorders

The best therapists adjust their techniques to accommodate individual and diverse learning styles. For example, I speak very dramatically and specifically when working with children with learning disorders to make sure they understand me. I frequently text patients between appointments to remind them of goals and help them remember their commitments. This is especially helpful for my patients with ADD, as they often forget what they need to do. I also break down my suggestions and thoughts and provide concrete advice and support. It's a true partnership, an approach that benefits children with learning and attention difficulties, as they require direct instruction about how to implement strategies and suggestions in their daily life. This kind of support is an extremely important part of the work I do in caring for patients and transforming their lives, as well as the lives of their families. Here are some key approaches that make a world of difference for children with neurocognitive challenges.

## Hands-On Approach

Patients with learning disorders, ADD, and ASD often have executive functioning (EF) deficits. Executive functioning is the skill that helps us complete tasks efficiently, manage paperwork, schedule appointments, and organize our assignments. I often say it is the secretary of our brain. Your child with neurocognitive challenges often falls short on all these tasks. They have trouble completing assignments on time, managing their time effectively, complying with daily routines, and showing up to their appointments. Often, these tasks have been so difficult to accomplish and students receive so much criticism from parents, teachers, and peers that they develop extreme anxiety around these tasks. It's heartbreaking to know about the experiences of these children who are called "lazy" and "irresponsible." They're accused of "not making an effort," and the worst part to see is that they end up believing all these hurtful assertions. In session, I often help my patient perform the tasks that they struggle with, whether it is reading a book, writing an essay, or composing an email to a teacher or peer. These activities help them get started on their work, learn how to advocate for support, and give them emotional care they need when they're feeling anxious. Importantly, this kind of hands-on care can work to undercut the narrative that they are not capable or irresponsible. Wonderfully, as we work together, they gain confidence in their skills and abilities.

Another technique I use is to refer students to a tutor or executive functioning coach who I know is capable, empathic, and highly skilled with this particular cohort of patients. I then work directly with that support person to coordinate care. Alex, a bright eleventh grader, did the bare minimum to pass his subjects. He never handed his work in on time and lied to his parents about his academic progress. Recognizing the need for intervention, I connected him to an executive functioning coach and personally engaged in the process. Together, we created a system in which Alex gave the coach access to his email, so we had real-time information about his assignments and homework. I collaborated with both Alex and the coach to help understand his difficulties and provide support in a concrete manner. One strategy involved encouraging Alex to let the coach know when he couldn't complete his work independently. The proactive approach paid off and Alex began excelling in school.

When I help patients with their work or advise their tutors, I often use scaffolding as a method of support. Scaffolding, as mentioned before, is a type of support in which you break down the task into chunks and give the student cues as they complete the work.

I love sitting alongside my patients as they engage in their work. This approach gives me a firsthand view of their progress, enabling me to witness their experiences (including moments of anxiety) and to provide direct assistance. I do this in segments: initially offering direct support in the office, then progressing to patients working independently or with a tutor while periodically checking in with me, and finally patients achieve complete independence.

### Advocacy and Team Approach

As mentioned earlier, children with neurocognitive challenges frequently work with a team of professionals. I often spearhead meetings with all team members to make sure we are collaborating and presenting the best treatment approach for my patient. It is essential to include parents and teachers in these meetings, as they are on the "front line" of their child's behaviors, triumphs, and failures. My focus is explaining to everyone involved how a particular student operates. This way, they can use that information to help serve in the patient's best interest. I frequently consult with parents and teachers regarding specific problems and behaviors and come up with strategies and interventions to help them manage more effectively. Simply put, team meetings are very, very effective.

I consulted with Charlie, a bubbly fourth grader and diagnosed him with ADD. Charlie was highly disruptive in the classroom, where he insisted on wearing his cap and sunglasses, voiced his negative opinions loudly, and refused to participate. I implemented and attended a series of team meetings with Charlie's parents, his teachers, and his therapist. Every month I checked in on Charlie's progress and created a treatment plan for him. We gave him a behavior modification program to improve his participation and reduce his negativity. Charlie knew we were meeting and appreciated the attention and support. At the end of the year, Charlie was a different student. He participated enthusiastically and no longer wore his cap and glasses.

Helping patients advocate for themselves and use the tools I have taught them independently takes a lot of work and support. I take a structured, sequential approach and help my patients move from working closely with me or their support people to working independently.

When I first began working with Michael, a bright, highly anxious ninth-grade student with learning disorder and ADD, we worked on his written assignments together. I gave him ideas about how to outline, read the material with him, and helped him organize his ideas. Initially, the work was painfully slow; Michael had trouble writing even one sentence! His anxiety was palpable, as he perspired and stuttered as we worked. With a lot of cheerleading, once we created the outline, Michael relaxed and began creating entire paragraphs fluently. As our work progressed, he began working with a tutor. Finally, after several years, Michael announced: "I am a good writer!"

This story of success is not unique to this student. When we understand how children learn, we can design an effective treatment that accommodates their style and enables them to succeed.

In sum, children with neurocognitive challenges do really well with specific treatment approaches that are tailored to accommodate their disorders. There are many effective treatment approaches such as psychoeducation, insight-oriented treatment, CBT, and DBT. I also highly recommend group therapy, as it is so helpful for children who struggle socially. Last but definitely not least is working with the parents and teachers who are the "boots on the ground" and who remain the most important influences.

## CHAPTER EIGHT

# PREPARING YOUR CHILD WITH
# NEUROCOGNITIVE CHALLENGES FOR COLLEGE

Going to college is often a daunting task for most students, neuro-typical or not, as it involves separation from family, a higher level of independence academically, socially, and emotionally, and an adjustment to a new environment. Children with neurocognitive challenges face all of these obstacles but with an added twist: their "hardwiring" is in most cases not set up for these new and increased demands. It is therefore essential that parents, teachers, therapists, and tutors all do their best to prepare these children for the demands of college life. In order to meaningfully prepare your child, you must understand the developmental expectations of each stage and what neurocognitive and emotional challenges might prevent your child from performing to the best of his or her ability.

Adolescents with neurocognitive challenges struggle with competency and friendships and therefore have fewer opportunities and options to spread their wings, try new things, and develop an appreciation of their own skills and capabilities. As a reaction to their learning and attention deficits, they are often anxious about their skills and can become quite perfectionistic and obsessive. Conversely, they may adopt a blasé attitude and say they don't care and don't want to do well because they feel they can't succeed. Both the anxious and apathetic students tend to avoid challenges, and their responses greatly hinder their ability to separate, adapt to new environments, and acquire the skills they need to succeed in college. With the proper support and intervention from parents, teachers, and clinicians, we can give these students the skills they need to flourish.

Sally, a high schooler with dyslexia whom I previously mentioned, is now in twelfth grade and getting ready for college. She works daily with her English and special education teachers to improve her reading and writing skills. They've set a goal with Sally to achieve independence by using the technology available to her such as speech-to-text, spell-check, and Grammarly. In addition, they have asked her to proofread her own work by reading it aloud to make sure it makes sense. Recently, Sally proudly announced that she had written and proofread a paper entirely on her own, using the skills taught to her by her teachers. She asked for help in pointing out sentences with errors and then painstakingly read them aloud in an attempt to fix her errors. She commented with determination, "I need to prepare for college and edit my own papers."

Emotionally being able to separate is a monumental task and requires an essential key ingredient: good self-esteem. Sadly, many children with neurocognitive challenges have terrible self-esteem. They feel awful about themselves, blaming their shortcomings on self-perceived faults. They've also been scarred by repetitive criticism from parents, peers, and teachers. As mentioned earlier, because they feel "stupid," "lazy," or both, repairing their self-esteem is critical for them to be able to separate. At the root of this is understanding that their problems are neurocognitive in nature. This is what will help them feel better about themselves, so offering them support and understanding in this area is crucial.

Leslie, our high schooler with nonverbal learning disorder (NVLD), was someone who expressed extreme anxiety about leaving her family and living with a roommate. Leslie's mother did all household chores for her including laundry and the dishes. Whenever Leslie tried to help, her mother would criticize her, saying, for example, "You're stacking the dishwasher wrong!" With this feedback, Leslie would retreat. Her mother didn't understand that Leslie's learning challenges made it hard for her to execute these tasks properly. With support from me, Leslie approached her mother and explained that she needed to learn how to do these things so she could adapt to college life. She was able to advocate for herself and explained to her mother that NVLD made it harder for her to do chores; she could do them, albeit more slowly and imperfectly. Leslie began doing her own laundry and cleaning the kitchen and felt very proud of her accomplishments.

As children with neurocognitive challenges get easily overwhelmed and feel insecure about their skills, preparing them for college should be done in a slow, steady manner. Each activity should be slowly and thoughtfully articulated and broken down into steps.

Sam was a serious student with ADD who struggled to work independently. When he came to see me, he was in twelfth grade and concerned about his readiness for college. He often procrastinated and did things at the last minute; he was anxious about this happening to him in college, where, as he put it, "I can't get away with it like high school." We began therapy by getting Sam to use a planner to plot out his long-term assignments. For essay writing, I taught Sam to estimate how much time each step—coming up with a topic, research, writing, and editing—would take. Once he understood all the steps, we started brainstorming how he could work independently. Sam worked well in the library, so he began staying after school to work there. Each and every step was methodically tracked and discussed. It took a long time to accomplish, but, along the way, Sam discussed his fears about college, and it was a wonderful opportunity to figure out how to help him improve his skills.

As parents and teachers, we need to understand the developmental expectations of young people in order to best support our teenagers as they move through late adolescence.

## IDENTITY DEVELOPMENT

According to Erik Erikson, an esteemed ego psychologist and pioneer in explicating adolescent development, adolescence is a time of identity development and formation.[1] Marsha Levy-Warren describes the three developmental stages of adolescence in her seminal book *The Adolescent Journey* this way: Early adolescence, she says, is when puberty begins and children respond to physical and hormonal changes with mood shifts, questioning authority, and establishing themselves with their peers. Middle adolescence is a time of figuring out sexual identity and beginning to cultivate interests outside of their narrow social group. Late adolescence is when young people step into adulthood with mature sexual relationships and establishing a coherent identity.[2]

Identity formation and development is a fraught process for children with neurocognitive challenges; this makes perfect sense because our identities are formed through succeeding at tasks and getting validation from others. As we know, children with neurocognitive challenges often fail at tasks, receiving far more than their fair share of criticism due to their disabilities. Identification with adults is another hallmark of identity development. Again, children with neurocognitive challenges can feel stymied in their quest to identify with others; they compare themselves unfavorably with peers and adults alike and despair of ever achieving anything remotely like they imagine success to be. Dealing with frustration, persevering, and eventually mastering a given task is another key element of identity development, but the ambitions of children with neurocognitive challenges are often thwarted. And because they don't have the experience of striving and succeeding, they're not learning how to persevere. All of these experiences lead to negative responses and emotional scars. In the next section, I elaborate on them so we can understand what is going on with our children and how best to intervene.

## IMPOSTER SYNDROME

Students with learning and attention difficulties often feel they are imposters and are "faking it." They feel as if they're "fooling" teachers, parents, and peers and worry that they'll be discovered as being "dumb" and "lazy." They can feel ashamed and often experience getting help such as tutoring or extended time on tests as "cheating." To cope with their neurocognitive challenges, they may have developed destructive strategies that involve lying to their parents about their work, hiding their disabilities from their peers, and avoiding challenging tasks. Hyper-aware, they're also deeply concerned about being failures in college. To help them succeed away from home, it is essential for them to learn new habits, retraining their brain to come up with constructive compensatory strategies. And of course, understanding where their feelings are coming from and debunking these myths that they have created about themselves is incredibly important in helping them get started on a successful path.

My patient Scott, an extraordinarily bright seventeen-year-old, was highly anxious and had difficulty eating and sleeping. My assessment uncovered previously undiagnosed dyslexia as well as depression. Scott was very relieved to hear this and tearfully confessed that he felt like a fraud. The truth was that Scott had never been able to complete a book but was able to achieve excellent grades because he "cheated" by skimming books and using SparkNotes as a crutch. I explained that these were brilliant compensatory strategies! I also helped him use some other strategies, such as listening to books on Audible and watching the movie versions of books.

When untreated, experiences like Scott's lead to intense shame and guilt that further hinder any ability to strategize and compensate for learning and attention difficulties. The shame is twofold: it is both humiliating to perform badly and embarrassing to be one of the lowest performers in the group. It is vitally important to address these issues head-on in high school and before college, when they are more on their own and without the safety net of home.

Alan, an anxious twelfth grader, constantly lied to his parents about overdue assignments and test grades. Although he was highly intelligent, he was at risk for failing high school because he had such difficulty showing up for class or doing his work. When I diagnosed him with attention deficit disorder (ADD), the first priority was honesty with me and his parents about his work. We discussed Alan's deep feelings of shame around his procrastination and his strong desire to succeed, even though he doubted his abilities and felt that he would never excel. Alan took a crucial first step toward establishing independence by openly sharing his anxiety with his parents.

## DEALING WITH FEELINGS

Due to hormonal and physical changes that are taking place in the body, adolescence is a time of intense emotions. Children with neurocognitive challenges have difficulty dealing with their feelings and are at a real disadvantage in this area. Teens with ADD can be impulsive, overreact to situations, and fly off the handle. Children with language-based learning disorders may have trouble communicating their feelings effectively and may get extra frustrated as a result. Teens with autism spectrum disorder (ASD) get easily overwhelmed by any intense kind of stimulus and are often ill equipped to deal with the typical emotional upheaval that accompanies adolescence. To cope, they often employ maladaptive strategies such as avoidance, blowing up, or being angry at themselves, thus falling short. Teachers and parents need to understand these responses and help their teens to express their feelings safely and effectively. A good therapist can play a vital role in assisting young people and helping them figure out better coping strategies that foster emotional well-being and resilience.

Jeremy, a talented sixteen-year-old boy, loved theater and had a close-knit group of friends. He did well in school and had a good relationship with his parents. Diagnosed with both ADD and ASD, he took medicine and received academic support. In therapy, he discussed his profound feelings of anger and disappointment with himself. He actually saw himself as a "failure" and was particularly preoccupied with his difficulty maintaining romantic relationships. Whenever he faced rejection in his dating life, he obsessively ruminated on his perceived shortcomings, engaging in self-deprecating thoughts and labeling himself negatively as a "loser." I told Jeremy that disappointment and frustration is a universal part of being human and emphasized that he too is a person who goes through these often felt, common emotions. Although initially skeptical and firm in his belief that he was correct in his self-assessment, I was gradually able to help him come to a more peaceful place when feeling disappointed.

## FAMILY RELATIONSHIPS

The tumultuousness of adolescence makes it a difficult time for the parent-child relationship. Teens are typically rebellious, and teens with neurocognitive challenges in particular can be very oppositional and withdrawn. They have more difficulty negotiating conflict and confrontation due to their learning and attention issues. If undiagnosed, their issues are often misinterpreted as unmotivated, lazy, and stubborn, further breaking down parent-child communication. Proper diagnosis and treatment can greatly help the family dynamic because parents begin to understand their child, which goes a long way in making those children feel more understood and supported.

## COLLEGE PREP PROGRAMS

There are many different summer experiences that can prepare adolescents for college. Children with neurocognitive challenges really benefit from exposure to the college environment as well as practicing those academic skills that they will need to succeed. In addition, going on a teen tour is a good opportunity to learn how to make new friends, adapt to new environments, and socialize in a group.

## FRIENDSHIPS

As we all know, social life is a huge part of college. Teens with neurocognitive challenges suffer socially for a myriad of reasons. Suffice it to say that learning and attention deficits interfere with socialization. It's important to provide our teens with both social coaching and new social experiences so they can improve these skills that are so necessary to college social life. Let's look at each disorder and the specific difficulties and remedies for these issues.

## LANGUAGE-BASED LEARNING DISORDER

As discussed in earlier chapters, children with language-based learning disorder struggle with words. Typically, reading complex stories and writing essays are frustrating and arduous for math and science kids who are adept at computers and technology. Socially, these students can feel insecure, as they may not be able to engage in the rapid banter of their peers. Emotionally, they can also be anxious about their deficits and saddened by their challenges.

Preparing them for college means being aware of these issues and providing support and intervention. Academic life involves reading and writing, thus specialized remediation in these areas is crucial for them. Helping them develop outside pursuits that facilitate self-esteem and socialization is another necessary step for separation and establishing identity. Finally, exposing them to new social experiences in small doses with coaching is a great antidote to their feelings of social anxiety. A coach, for example, may suggest that they join a club based on a common interest, volunteer at a community-based organization, or participate in community events to help widen their social network. The coach would work with them on strategies to socialize while they participate in these events.

## NONVERBAL LEARNING DISORDER

As mentioned in earlier chapters, students with NVLD are fantastic with words but have real trouble with visual information such as numbers and maps. They have difficulty with time management, keeping track of their assignments, and cleaning their room. Socially, they can be perceived as awkward, as they may have difficulty responding to nonverbal cues such as body language. Emotionally, they are at risk for anxiety and depression.

Academic support is essential for these students to improve their mastery of math and science skills. In addition, the use of a planner and other organization strategies will help them become comfortable with sticking to a schedule and handing in assignments on a timely basis. Socially, they require coaching on observing body language to be able to judge if people with whom they engage are uncomfortable.

## ATTENTION DEFICIT DISORDER

As we all know, teens with ADD are incredibly impulsive and easily distracted. Academically, they suffer from their short attention span, need for frequent movement, and tangential thoughts. It is so hard for them to pay attention in class, complete homework assignments, and participate. Socially, they may also struggle for similar reasons; they can be "flaky," inconsistent, and disorganized. They often miss social engagements. Emotionally, they may feel frustrated, have low self-esteem, and feel insecure about their capabilities.

The number one priority for kids with ADD is to improve their organizational skills by giving them academic support and tools such as a planner, use of technology, and reminders to use Post-it notes or a whiteboard. Socially and behaviorally, these students benefit from interventions designed to reduce their impulsivity so they are more aware of their tendency to interrupt and not listen and can put in the effort needed to engage in conversation.

## AUTISM SPECTRUM DISORDER

Teens with ASD are at a serious social disadvantage, as they have such difficulty understanding other people's perspectives. In addition, they are extremely rigid, which can be very off-putting to others. Moreover, they may exhibit mannerisms like poor eye contact and rocking behaviors. These actions can give the impression that they're uninterested in making friends, even if they genuinely desire social contact. Their rigidity also makes it hard for them to adjust to new situations and environments. They often have a fairly unemotional demeanor that seems flat to peers, and they can't express their feelings in an unfettered manner.

To prepare for college, teens with ASD require a great deal of coaching and support, particularly in social situations. Helping them understand somebody else's perspective requires a lot of patience and creativity. Breaking down the back-and-forth of an interpersonal exchange can be illuminating to them. For example, watching a TV show or movie while explaining the motives behind the characters' actions can be really helpful. Additionally, social flexibility improves with gradual exposure to new situations in short spurts of time.

Worried about their daughter's prospects for success in college, Jade's parents reached out to me when she was in twelfth grade. A socially anxious, withdrawn young woman who enjoyed drawing and swimming, Jade was described by her parents as very rigid. She preferred to adhere to a consistent daily schedule and needed a lot of "downtime" alone in her room. After I assessed and diagnosed her with ASD, I recommended to both Jade and her parents that they incorporate a new activity into her routine each week, dedicating thirty minutes to it. To ensure her success, we initially discussed the upcoming activity and set clear parameters for her engagement. In order to gradually expand her social interactions, for example, Jade started exploring various parts of her neighborhood. I further encouraged her by suggesting activities that involved interacting with people. Consequently, Jade joined the swim team, which led to new social experiences and, importantly, new friendships. These collective experiences served as valuable preparation for her eventual transition to college.

## COLLEGE LIFE WHEN YOU ARE NEUROCOGNITIVELY CHALLENGED: HOW TEACHERS AND PARENTS CAN BE A SOURCE OF SUPPORT

Neurocognitive challenges do not magically disappear once you enter college. In fact, for most students, higher education means higher demands. Therefore, it's extremely important that we understand how to support students throughout their college journey. To succeed, students must be mature self-starters who are able to take initiative and advocate for themselves.

### Planning Ahead Is Essential to Ensure Success

The first step is choosing the appropriate college environment for your student. For kids with neurocognitive challenges, that can be very complicated. First off, we need to be concerned about the fit of the college for the student, rather than how "good" the college is for everyone else. There are colleges that are better prepared than others to accommodate students with neurocognitive challenges. These schools have excellent learning centers, access to accommodations, and sophisticated advisers to guide the student in course selection. Socially, the fit is important as well. As mentioned previously, these students can struggle interpersonally, so finding a warm, supportive community is extremely important.

The next step is to establish appropriate accommodations and make sure the student is receiving them. In college, students are required to submit their neuropsychological evaluations to the office of student disabilities. They then need to determine the necessary steps to receive accommodations. This may involve direct communication with professors or coordination with the office of disabilities. Regardless of the method, it is crucial for students to effectively advocate for their accommodation needs in order to guarantee their implementation. Given the challenges that students with neurocognitive issues may face in organizational and administrative tasks, providing them with support to do this is essential. In addition to the organizational chops required to get their accommodations running smoothly, college youth may have negative feelings about the accommodations themselves. My college patients often tell me how humiliated they feel about getting accommodations. They feel singled out and even undeserving of the accommodations. They view the accommodations as "cheating" and express a desire to be more independent, meaning that they don't need the accommodations. Some students go so far as to completely reject all accommodations and support, because they want to "do it on their own." Sadly, they often fail or come close to failure because they reject help and support. Here is an example of one such student with ADD.

Alex, a very bright first-year college student, had been diagnosed with ADD in twelfth grade. He had significant difficulty going to class and completing assignments on time. I designed an intervention plan for him that included medication, tutoring, academic support, and accommodations such as reduced course load and extended time on tests and assignments. With these supports, he—who had been at risk of failing out—was able to graduate high school. When he entered college, he announced that he wanted to be independent, refusing regular meetings with his tutor and organizational coach. He also stopped taking his medicine regularly and then ceased going to class or doing any type of schoolwork. When he finally told me about the situation, I immediately wrote to his adviser regarding his ADD and anxiety and asked for extended time on his late assignments. Dropping two classes, Alex focused on completing the other three. With renewed medication and support, he was able to pass.

Important accommodations to consider are extended time on testing and assignments, testing in a small, quiet location, reduced course load, priority registration, access to academic and organizational support, a language waiver, access to notes, a note taker, a quiet environment, social coaching via a peer mentor program, and an adviser to help navigate the system. These accommodations are keys to success. When implemented properly, they make a huge difference in the lives of college students with neurocognitive challenges. Here's a look at how accommodations help students with neurocognitive disorders.

## Nonverbal Learning Disorder

Leslie, our student with NVLD, entered college with a plethora of accommodations, including the two most important: extended time on tests and testing in a separate, quiet location. However, initially she did not make use of them. In order to get what she needed, Leslie had to approach each professor directly, ask them for the extended time accommodation, and then go to the office with disabilities to arrange a proctored test. These logistical steps were a nightmare for Leslie so instead she simply tried to take her tests with everybody else. What a bad idea that was! She consistently ran out of time and her grades tanked. To help her, we role-played the act of going to both the professor's office and the office of disabilities. With my support, Leslie was able to master her anxiety and approached the school successfully. Her grades dramatically improved!

## Autism Spectrum Disorder

Jade was diagnosed with ASD in high school and experienced debilitating anxiety around academics and social interactions. A very important accommodation for her was a reduced course load. Jade started out in college taking one class to get accustomed to the workload and gradually increased her course load over the next year. Another accommodation was a quiet room with low lighting where Jade could go when she felt overstimulated. Access to this room was essential to help her in transitions between classes. She was delighted with the slow entry and commented, "I am so happy I got through each semester without having to withdraw due to stress. I was able to take classes at my own pace!"

## Learning Disorder and Attention Deficit Disorder

Rachel, a bright college student with ADD and learning disorder could not keep up with taking notes in class. She was so appreciative when the school designated one student to share her notes with her in each class. She commented, "Now I can really listen in class and not worry about taking down every word." She was able to easily coordinate with the designated students and had good communication with them about the classroom material.

## WHAT HAPPENS AFTER ACCOMMODATIONS ARE IN PLACE?

### How Can We Support Students Socially and Emotionally?

Once we are able to establish a good plan and the student is well supported academically, we need to pay attention to their social and emotional lives. As I mentioned, students with neurocognitive challenges have complex emotional responses to both their disorders and the help that they need to succeed because of those disorders. Though they may feel out of step with their peers in taking a reduced course load, it's important to reassure them that there is no one way to get through college. Even when we think students with neurodiversity have accepted their difficulties, feelings of shame and frustration continue to arise on a regular basis. For them, it remains truly challenging to get their work done. With so much stress, they remain vulnerable to avoiding work entirely.

I learned how embarrassed my patient with ADD and learning disorder felt about her academic skills when I asked her how her plans to write a paper over the weekend went. She reacted by flying into a rage, accusing me of being insensitive and of asking a "fucked up" question. As we discussed her outburst, we understood that she felt shamed by my questioning her about her work as she "felt SPED" (special education) and incompetent. It took time to help her recognize that she was both very bright and had learning and attention disorders that made it extremely hard for her to do her work. Once she accepted this truth, she was able to feel less ashamed and more confident about her skills.

Socially, patients with neurocognitive challenges often suffer in college as they have throughout their academic lives. To recap, students with language-based learning disorders have difficulty engaging in the rapid banter of their peers. Students with ADD may alienate peers with impulsive comments or "flaking" out on commitments. Students with

ASD can be quite rigid, and have trouble emoting and understanding others' perspectives. Students with NVLD can be perceived as "flighty" and disorganized. Many students with neurocognitive challenges suffer from social anxiety as well. Anecdotally, many of my patients have reported being bullied due to their lack of social competence, which of course only adds to their anxiety and possible avoidance of social situations.

To facilitate social success, both individual and group therapy can be extremely helpful. Individual therapy provides a forum to discuss social situations and improve anxiety symptoms. Group therapy helps practice social skills in the here and now and also provides peers with whom to commiserate and learn from. I run a group for young adults with neurocognitive challenges, and it is an extremely effective treatment to reduce social anxiety. The patients understand the impact of learning and attention disorders, support each other's challenges, and help one another move forward in their lives.

In a recent group meeting, one member, Adam, poignantly discussed how ashamed he is of his executive functioning issues, particularly his slowed speed. He lamented how long it takes him to absorb new material and how hard he has to work at his job. Another member, Emily, commented that it was not his fault, but rather society's. She shared how she came to understand that there was nothing wrong with the way she learned. She was able to learn anything; she just needed to be taught differently and it took more time. This discussion was extremely productive for all members, who reflected on their different learning styles, commiserated with the frustration, and affirmed their inherent value.

In addition to therapy, participation in clubs at college is a great way to make friends based on common interests or a shared identity. Social coaching via a peer mentorship program can be a very effective way to improve skills and make friends. I also encourage my students to participate in group outings and events and help them prepare by role-playing how to make small talk.

Leslie, the student with NVLD mentioned earlier, was super-shy and unable to make friends at college. Because she identifies as gay, I suggested we research the lesbian club at her college. It took us months, but Leslie finally attended a club event. Although she stayed only a short time, over the next year, she started attending the club regularly, where she socialized with the group and established a close circle of friends.

### What Happens When the College Student Fails?

Sadly, students with neurocognitive challenges are vulnerable to failing their classes and dropping out of college even with a lot of support. As I mentioned earlier, failures are most common when students are not utilizing their resources. If this happens, it may be best to take a medical leave, which is permission granted to temporarily suspend college attendance until a student recovers. This can be an important option for some students who are totally overwhelmed by the academic and social demands and need time to regroup, get support, and figure out a better plan going forward. Sometimes, transferring to a different school with more support or returning to home is also a good option. In these cases, it's important to reassure the student that he or she can succeed, but merely in a different environment. Often, it is simply too much for students to juggle independence—taking care of themselves and dealing with college. They need the support of home to help them transition to college life. When Leslie first went to college, she left home, became extremely depressed, and was unable to attend class. I put in a medical leave for her, and she transferred to a college where she took classes and lived with her parents. In this way she was able to be very successful and graduated with good grades and a nice group of friends. I explain to my patients that not all students need to leave home to go to college. We need to determine the best fit for each unique individual; a cookie-cutter approach is not the answer.

## DRUGS AND ALCOHOL

Students with ADHD are considered an at-risk group for substance and alcohol use due to their impulsivity and challenges with emotional control; they may turn to substances impulsively. Similarly, students with learning difficulties are at risk because they often have low self-esteem and are socially anxious, which drives them to drink or experiment with drugs, especially in social situations. It's imperative to engage in open, honest conversations with our children about alcohol and drugs, providing them with knowledge about the symptoms of overuse.

In sum, I want to emphasize that you absolutely can help your child with neurocognitive challenges succeed in college. It is important to remember that there is no one right way to get through this important period of one's life. You can come up with a specific plan for your child that is designed to help compensate for his or her difficulties and to help him or her thrive! Making sure that such students have the appropriate accommodations and resources is half the battle. The other half is helping them succeed socially and emotionally. There are many resources and much support available in college for the students who seek and need help. In the next chapter, we discuss the impact of COVID, sibling relationships, and cultural concerns.

## CHAPTER NINE

# SPECIAL ISSUES

This chapter is devoted to topical issues that impact children with neurocognitive challenges. Here I discuss the effects of COVID, cultural concerns, screen time regulation, and balancing sibling relationships. In addition, I provide resources for special needs families and highlight the positive aspects of each challenge.

## THE IMPACT OF COVID AND REMOTE LEARNING

The COVID-19 pandemic was devastating for many children, especially those with neurocognitive challenges. School closures, social isolation, and remote learning removed kids from their regular routines, deprived them of access to peers and teachers, and reduced their access to support services; it was deeply debilitating. Children with neurocognitive challenges were especially hard hit by these problems because they rely on the structured routines provided by school, require interaction with peers for socialization, and heavily depend on support services to help them with their specific challenges. There was also a notable rise in depression and anxiety among children and adolescents in response to the social isolation, boredom, and remote learning. However, there are children and adolescents who thrived during COVID-19 due to the slowed pace of life, less pressure (both social and academic), and more family time. In a bit, I discuss the reasons why most children suffered during COVID. I also analyze those who thrived and offer some reasons why, during the same time, they flourished. The phenomenon known as the "COVID slide" describes an overall decrease in academic skills among school-age children during the pandemic. This slide was most dramatically exhibited by students already in the lowest performing group.

There are many factors that contributed to the slide, including the loss of physical activity and an increase in sedentary behaviors (including screen time), which led to depression, poor academic performance, and obesity. Social isolation hits teenagers the hardest because adolescence is a time of learning about relationships and being part of a group, which is why depression and anxiety were also pronounced during this time.

## Why Did Children with Learning Disorders Suffer the Most during COVID?

*Learning Disorders*

Children with learning disorders face specific challenges in understanding material presented on Zoom. They have trouble paying attention and struggle without direct feedback from their teachers to help them with the material. This creates a vicious cycle: without understanding the material and getting help from teachers, they get stressed out about their performance and avoid academic work entirely, leading to even more academic difficulties!

As discussed earlier in the book, children with language-based learning disorders do best in classrooms with direct one-to-one instruction, something that cannot be replicated on Zoom. In addition, children with learning disorders frequently struggle to keep up with their peers under normal, non-pandemic social circumstances. But when these children lack regular interactions with friends, their social skills decline, leading to heightened feelings of anxiety and depression. Meet Sarah, an introspective, artistic twelve-year-old girl who consulted with me due to her parents' concern that she was "dreamy and moody" during COVID. Sarah explained to me that she has dyslexia and went to a special education school. She told me that she felt excluded from her peers because remote learning prevented any socialization. She felt hesitant and anxious about reaching out to classmates and missed the regular classroom routine that provided "easy" social contact.

*Attention Disorders*

Children with attention deficit hyperactivity disorder (ADHD) thrive on structure and routine, making the disruptions caused by COVID particularly difficult for them. Given their challenges with focusing in a traditional school setting, you can imagine that their home environments are even more distracting! Don't forget that kids with ADD really need physical activity, so the loss of activity during the pandemic also greatly contributed to depression and anxiety. Because children with attention deficit disorder (ADD) rely on athletic activities to channel their energy, the lack of scheduled sports and outdoor time was very stressful. Carter, an eight-year-old boy, consulted with me because of his poor grades, uncooperative attitude, and refusal to do any activities. Carter's parents told me that before the pandemic, he was lively and energetic. However, he was unable to pay attention during Zoom learning and could focus only when an adult was sitting next to him. He became difficult and lethargic. Carter told me school was "hard" and "boring." He said he missed going to class and wanted to see his friends. I diagnosed Carter with ADD. Once he started medicine and teletherapy, he began to adjust well to remote learning.

Children with ADD are more "at risk" of becoming addicted to screens because their brains are wired to respond to immediate feedback and instant gratification. During the pandemic, screen addiction became even more prevalent because children were on the computer all day with fewer, if any, activities after school. I have seen an increase in parents reporting screen-addicted children both during and after the pandemic.

*Autism Spectrum Disorder*

Children with autism spectrum disorder (ASD) are particularly wedded to routine and structure. In general, they're extremely rigid and averse to transitions. You can imagine that the pandemic was disruptive for children with ASD because they're so reliant on routines and prone to anxiety. Interestingly, children with ASD can easily become anxious and obsessive about health, so COVID was especially triggering for them. These health concerns are related to their overall fears about their body and lack of confidence in their health. Last, being at home with families who may lack understanding or struggle to manage their unique challenges added to the difficulties faced by children with ASD during the pandemic.

Adam, a sweet, shy fifteen-year-old boy with ASD had a terrible response to COVID. Before the pandemic, he attended school and had a circle of friends with whom he hung out. However, when school went remote, he refused to go to classes, isolated himself from family and friends, and ruminated about his fear of getting sick. He was so anxious about COVID that he strenuously avoided all contact with people. During our teletherapy sessions, we were able to discuss his fears, and Adam was able to return to class and, importantly, learned to socialize online with his friends.

### Silver Linings

In addition to some of the negative effects, there were also silver linings for children and teens during the pandemic. Spending more time with family helped children and adolescents feel better about themselves and more supported by their loved ones. Parents noticed improved eating and sleeping habits, which may have been because children were better supervised. The reduced academic pressure allowed for more time to pursue hobbies and pastimes. Children had the opportunity to engage in reading for pleasure, picking up a new musical instrument, or discovering and pursuing new interests. Children who are socially anxious found relief from the absence of those daunting social pressures in school. Additionally, for those who experienced bullying, the break from school provided a welcome opportunity to distance themselves from the toxic atmosphere and find a temporary respite.

I saw firsthand the silver lining with children who were able to relax, feel better about themselves, and appreciate the slower pace of pandemic life. Meet Zoe, a thirteen-year-old girl with dyslexia and ADD, whose mother, Jane, reported a dramatic change in her behavior at home during the pandemic. Although Zoe was a sweet, cooperative, hard-working student, at home she would become moody and very agitated, especially around homework. During the pandemic, she and her mother went to the countryside, where Zoe took her classes remotely and Jane provided a great deal of hands-on support. Zoe responded to this attention and care by relaxing, expressing positive feelings about homework (a first!), and going on long nature hikes. Zoe reported that she had developed an appreciation of nature and felt more comfortable with herself.

## Teletherapy

During COVID, remote learning became so widely accepted because it was considered the only safe option. Currently, many therapists and patients still use platforms like Zoom or the phone for remote sessions. I prefer to be with my patients in person; it affords the therapist the opportunity to connect with the patient more deeply, and there's so much information gained by being in the physical presence of another person. Additionally, therapists can develop "screen fatigue," as it is exhausting to focus on the small screen for long periods of time. Last, both therapist and patient can be distracted by email, texts, and online entertainment. However, the reality is that many patients opt for remote sessions because it's far more convenient. Nonetheless, for children with special needs, the research is clear that teletherapy is effective.[1]

## Ripple Effects

Currently, we have moved beyond lockdown, back to pre-COVID life. However, the pandemic's impact on the academic skills and mental health of our children continues to be felt. For children with neurocognitive challenges, this impact is significant. The social isolation and pandemic-related anxiety and depression exacerbated the neurocognitive deficits and mental health problems demonstrated by special needs children. In order to effectively intervene on behalf of our at-risk children, we need to step up our academic and emotional care. Providing one-on-one academic support is crucial for helping kids catch up on the academic skills they may have fallen behind on during the pandemic. Additionally, therapeutic intervention is another key component in enhancing children's mental health.

Now, let's shift focus to address the cultural and racial concerns of families with special needs children.

## CULTURAL CONCERNS

Race and class differences influence families raising children with neurocognitive challenges on every level. Access to resources is a major concern as therapy, testing, and special services are often expensive and may not be covered by insurance. Lower income or minority families may feel misunderstood and uncomfortable because the professionals working with them may come from dissimilar backgrounds. It is crucial for professionals to demonstrate cultural sensitivity and remain mindful of differences. Interestingly, each disorder presents differently in terms of cultural, racial, and socioeconomic differences. Let's take a look.

### Attention Deficit Disorder (ADD)

ADD in children is thought to be diagnosed in 10 percent of the population. However, minority children are frequently underdiagnosed so it's imperative that minority families be extra vigilant and proactive in advocating for their children. Parents themselves may be unaware of the impact of ADD on their kids and react punitively. My experiences with Carter and his family illustrate this issue.

An adorable, exuberant eight-year-old African American boy, Carter was brought into my office by his parents who were concerned about his impulsivity and aggression. In school and at home, Carter had difficulty cooperating with routines, frequently drifted off during class, and had temper tantrums when frustrated. Carter's parents, horrified with his behavior, took a strict disciplinary approach, which resulted in more tears and tantrums from Carter. Testing revealed ADD and I recommended medicine, therapy, and academic support. Carter's parents did not want to medicate him, so we embarked on parent guidance sessions and academic support. During the family sessions, Carter's parents were able to let go of their previous conceptions of Carter as "bad" and began to understand his neurological issues with impulse control and frustration tolerance. Once we instituted a behavior management system at home and in school, Carter's behaviors improved. His father tearfully told me, "I think I have ADD as well and I feel so guilty about the way I treated Carter." Both Carter and his father started on ADD medication with good results.

### Learning Disorders

Approximately 10 percent of children in the United States have learning disabilities. Similar to ADHD, there are wide disparities in disability identification by race and ethnicity. However, the statistics on learning disorders reflect a very different pattern than ADHD. Whereas students of color are underrepresented among children diagnosed with attention disorders, they notably are overrepresented among children diagnosed with learning disabilities. Thus, minority families whose children are diagnosed with learning disorders often need to advocate that their children remain in the mainstream instead of getting shunted off to special education classes where they are not receiving appropriate support.

My experiences working with minority families underscored this issue. I often encountered children who were in special education classes and were horrifyingly illiterate because they had not received the type of academic support appropriate to their learning style. "Social promotion" is when the school promotes a child because he is too old to be left back but lacks the academic skills to enter the next grade. Sadly, many schools keep on promoting these children, a tremendous disservice, as it deprives children of the one-on-one instruction they need most. As I strenuously advocated to get my minority patients with learning disorders the one-on-one support they deserved, their academic skills dramatically improved.

## Bilingualism

Fluency in two languages is an amazing accomplishment! Giving your child the gift of bilingualism is commendable. However, children with learning and attention challenges often struggle to master one language, let alone two! Because learning languages requires memory skills, attention capacities, and language abilities, many children with ADD and learning disorders are not able to sufficiently express themselves or understand conversation. It's worth mentioning that neurocognitive challenges are sometimes more readily identified in bilingual children, as they are presented with a double load, so their difficulties are more clearly delineated. Teachers, therapists, and families need to be sensitive to the specific issues that bilingual children confront and how to support them most effectively. Obviously, it's ideal to conduct testing and therapy in a child's native language to ensure that they feel most comfortable and understood. However, when this isn't possible, we use interpreters. Best practice would be to use a professional interpreter rather than a family member to avoid potential conflicts and ensure accurate communication.

The story of seven-year-old Charlotte, a playful first grader, shows the pitfalls of a monolingual assessment of a bilingual child. Charlotte was referred to me by her teacher, who recognized Charlotte's academic struggles and trouble focusing in class. My testing confirmed these observations, and I explained to Charlotte's parents that she demonstrated both learning and attention difficulties. The parents contested the report and said they felt Charlotte was underperforming in school and in my office because she was more comfortable in Spanish. They saw Charlotte as a highly verbal girl who did not have trouble focusing when talking in Spanish. I offered to reassess Charlotte with an interpreter, and indeed she performed better in Spanish on the verbal tasks although she still demonstrated difficulties with focus. I recommended a bilingual classroom for Charlotte, as Spanish was her preferred language.

### Autism Spectrum Disorder

One in thirty-four children in the United States has autism. Similar to ADHD, the diagnosis and treatment of minority children with ASD lags behind white children. Minority children are often perceived as more assertive, and their behavioral challenges may be classified as conduct disorder rather than ASD. In general, boys are overrepresented in children with ASD. It's possible that girls are more socially aware, can better assimilate, and effectively "mask" their symptoms more successfully. As aggressive, early intervention is key to help improve the developing child's brain, it is really important for parents and teachers to be educated about the indicators of autism so they can promptly seek help for their children at a young age.

Now that we understand the prevalence of each disorder, I turn to specific issues of concern to families of special needs children. One issue I hear about regularly is how to negotiate screen time with children. Although this is an issue for all families in this day and age, effective strategies for managing screen time can be particularly challenging for families with children with neurocognitive challenges. How can parents implement appropriate limits and promote healthy screen habits?

### SCREEN TIME

Kids with ADD are more prone to getting addicted to video games and computer activities. This is because kids with ADD have real trouble with impulse control and tend to enjoy activities with instant gratification. Video games are designed to create an addictive experience for children who are helpless to resist them. It is a multimillion dollar business that is built on creating games that are impossible to put down. In my practice, I often encounter desperate parents who beg me to help them regulate their children's computer use and gaming.

Charley's parents came to consult with me because they were concerned about his obsessive gaming. An engaging, curly-haired fifteen-year-old, Charley told me that he spent every waking moment playing games. He gamed far into the night, often oversleeping, and was late for school. In a vain attempt to get him to shut down his computer, Charley's parents would go so far as to engage in physical altercations with him; once or twice they even called the police to scare him into compliance. My assessment of Charley revealed severe undiagnosed ADD. When medicated properly, Charley has been better able to regulate his gaming, and he is back to getting to school on time!

Kids with ASD often exhibit a hallmark trait of rigidity, making transitions from one activity to another extremely difficult. They can also be very obsessive and single-minded, a combination that makes limiting screen time a real challenge. An important principle for kids with ADD and ASD is consistency and routine. When you establish consistent structure and habits, your children will comply. Setting reasonable limits for each activity is the key for a successful evening and relationship. I encourage parents to set a few basic rules, such as prohibiting gaming before homework, ensuring that all screens are removed from children's bedrooms by a certain hour, and placing limits on the types of games that can be played.

I first met Jack and his three younger brothers during the COVID pandemic. Their parents were extremely concerned about Jack's dedication to video games, especially during the peak of social isolation. Although they generally succeeded in persuading the three younger boys to power down their screens and engage in screenless activities at dinner, Jack resisted. It often took an hour of intense negotiation, occasionally culminating in physical intervention, to get him to turn off the screen. My assessment revealed that Jack had ASD with a rigidity that was contributing to these significant, everyday conflicts. Jack entered therapy with medication, and his parents started parent guidance. Parent guidance is when the parents consult with an expert to help them parent more effectively. They instituted a strict schedule for computer time, allowing it only as a weekend reward. With these changes, Jack developed new hobbies like cooking and music, contributing to a much calmer and more harmonious family environment.

## SIBLINGS

As we all know, siblings play a very significant role in our lives. Having a sibling with neurocognitive challenges can be a source of significant distress. For parents, balancing the competing needs of neurodivergent and neurotypical children in one family can strain their patience, budget, and resources. However, there are also benefits for siblings in special needs families. These include increased maturity and flexibility, heightened compassion for others, and an enhanced appreciation of diversity. Therapeutic intervention for special needs families can be essential in helping siblings come to terms with negative feelings about their neurocognitively diverse siblings. Therapy with other siblings in a similar family dynamic can be a powerful tool, as children can comfort and empathize with each other. Feeling isolated and embarrassed by having a special needs sibling is common, and groups can alleviate the sting of feeling alone and unsupported.

Raphael, a sweet, exuberant eight-year-old boy whose older brother, Jake, had ASD, came into therapy because he was highly anxious, especially at night. In fact, Raphael required an elaborate bedtime routine in order to go to sleep. Raphael was sad that his brother could not play with him the way he wanted him to, and he also resented the amount of time and attention his brother demanded; he tearfully disclosed that he felt left out when his parents were occupied with taking care of Jake. Through therapy, he learned how to tell his parents how he felt and participate in activities with his brother. For example, the two brothers were able to engage in art together, watch favorite shows, and listen to books. His parents shared that Raphael was much calmer and his sleep habits improved.

Just as having a special needs sibling has positive benefits, being neurodivergent also has many valuable aspects. Celebrating our children's unique strengths and assets is essential to helping them flourish and thrive as children and adults. The next section describes the celebration of neurodivergence.

## EMBRACING NEURODIVERSITY

Today, those with neurodiversity embrace their differences and understand how it contributes to their unique talents. In addition, adults of all ages are actively involved in communities that promote and cultivate a profound sense of pride in their individual identities. Parents and teachers who work with children with neurocognitive challenges can turn to these communities for role models and inspiration. As more public figures speak out, there is also more representation on television and in books and films, a terrific change that has considerably helped overcome the stigma and shame associated with neurodiversity.

Sally, our high schooler with dyslexia who has been mentioned throughout the book, expressed comfort and acceptance of her disability. She felt at ease with her accommodations and had no problem advocating for herself. Sally's mother attributed her special education school for fostering positivity about dyslexia. "The school was so professional. They explained that people with dyslexia can be incredibly successful and always provided role models for the students." In my practice, I always welcome the opportunity to tell patients and their families about the positive aspects of various learning challenges. To provide empowering insights is one of the most gratifying aspects of my professional life. Now let's look further into the positive aspects of each disorder.

### Embracing Dyslexia

When you are dyslexic, you visualize the world in unexpected ways. The letter *b* can become a *d* or a *p*; this shows how the dyslexic brain is able to manipulate images and see the world from different perspectives. This is why so many people with dyslexia are creative and artistic! In fact, many famous artists such as Leonardo da Vinci, Pablo Picasso, and Andy Warhol were thought to be dyslexic. People with dyslexia are very talented at visual-spatial thinking and can excel in business, entrepreneurship, computers, and math. Although they read slowly, they think "outside the box" and can quickly and intuitively make connections that help them succeed. Famous people with dyslexia include Walt Disney, Ansel Adams, Charles Schwab, Cher, Harry Belafonte, and so many more. People with dyslexia do well in creative and artistic fields such as graphic design, architecture, and advertising.

As parents, it is important to keep our children's strengths in mind and help them celebrate their creativity even as we recognize the challenges of being neurodiverse. Jade's mother, Renee, consulted with me about parenting her sweet sixteen-year-old daughter with significant dyslexia and ADD. Jade was also a talented artist who excelled in drawing and design. I counseled Renee to help Jade connect with her artistic ability and take pride in her accomplishments even though academic tasks, including reading and writing, were challenging for her. Jade frequently expressed frustration and became distressed, particularly when she lost objects that were precious to her, such as AirPods. Her memory was so poor that she was prone to losing things frequently, such as earrings, homework assignments, and so forth. Recently, Renee recounted that Jade was very distressed upon losing her fourth pair of AirPods. Renee tried to console her but to no avail. She left the house and returned home to observe that Jade had painted a gorgeous picture of a pigeon. Renee commented to Jade, "Look how your brain works; you are so artistic, and you see the whole picture although you have trouble remembering details." Jade smiled and said, "I know, Mommy. I wish my memory was better but that is how my brain works and I am proud I am an artist."

### Celebrating ADD

The most significant aspect of those with ADD is their boundless energy. They have restless and inquiring minds. Rather than relying on the tried-and-true way of doing things, they are true pioneers, explorers, leaders, and visionaries. People with ADD tend to be spontaneous and thrive on excitement, making them extremely fun to be around and suited for jobs that require flexibility, moving around, and engaging in different types of activities. Simply put, they are the life of the party! Famous people with ADD include Albert Einstein and Pablo Picasso. Individuals with ADD tend to retain a childlike sense of humor and joy that facilitates professional and personal development. They are well suited for many jobs, including dance/music therapists, entrepreneurs, and aerobics instructors.

### Taking Pride in ASD

People with ASD have a superpower: their superb attention to detail and unflagging commitment to their passions. They are people who are able to sit and focus for long periods of time on activities that are quite taxing. For example, computer coding is ideally suited to people with ASD. Also, they have an incredible ability for single-minded focus and commitment, which helps them achieve their goals. Bobby Fischer harnessed his powers of focus and foresight to become an international chess grandmaster, winning his first of eight U.S. championship titles at the age of fourteen. Anthony Hopkins is another illustrious figure with ASD; he parlayed his talents into becoming a six-time Academy Award–winning actor. Last, individuals with ASD typically think in visual images, so they are natural graphic artists, cartoonists, and experts in digital presentation and art.

### Finding Joy in NVLD

People with nonverbal learning disorder (NVLD) are often highly verbal and analytical. Their facility with words makes them a natural at all jobs and pursuits that focus on language, such as education, law, and psychology. Although they may miss details, they are able to analyze a situation as a whole, easily plan ahead, and are master strategists. They also are skilled at taking other people's perspectives and are very empathetic.

Leslie, a young adult with NVLD, often lamented that she was a "bad roommate" because she was messy and didn't pull her weight around the house that she shared with her roommate, who would become disconcerted and agitated when Leslie unexpectedly came home early to use the bathroom when the roommate was showering. She thoughtfully observed that her roommate was also neurodivergent and got distressed regarding unexpected change. She noted that her roommate was upset about the holidays and detailed a plan she made to celebrate with them. I commented that being attuned to her roommate's needs and being able to plan to celebrate with them was far superior to washing the dishes. She smiled and said, "I can get someone to wash the dishes for me, but only I can help my roommate emotionally."

## RESOURCES FOR SPECIAL NEEDS FAMILIES

### Dyslexia

- *Everyone Reading* (https://everyonereading.org). Originating as the New York branch of the International Dyslexia Association forty years ago, the organization has evolved into a leading provider of professional development and support services, working to combat the stigma surrounding dyslexia and learning disorders. Everyone Reading is dedicated to empowering individuals with dyslexia and related learning disabilities to excel as readers, writers, and spellers by providing essential resources. Through expert professional development, parental support, and advocacy efforts, Everyone Reading strives to improve educational systems and foster a more inclusive environment for individuals with dyslexia and related learning disabilities.
- *International Dyslexia Association* (https://dyslexiaida.org). A nonprofit organization based in Pikesville, Maryland, focusing on dyslexia-related matters, International Dyslexia Association (IDA) boasts a membership exceeding nine thousand and more than forty branches across the United States and Canada, alongside global partnerships in twenty-one countries. IDA serves individuals with dyslexia, their families, and professionals. Through various initiatives like information dissemination, advocacy, and teacher training, IDA aims to support those with dyslexia and advocate for accommodations within educational and legislative frameworks.
- *Orton-Gillingham Academy* (www.ortonacademy.org). Originating in the early twentieth century, the Orton-Gillingham method is a multisensory phonics method for reading remediation. Emphasizing direct, explicit, cognitive, cumulative, and multisensory techniques, it's not only beneficial for individuals with dyslexia but also effective for all learners. Widely endorsed in the United States by more than fifteen commercial programs and numerous private schools

specializing in dyslexia and related learning differences, it aids in reading, spelling, and writing skills development for diverse learners.

- The *Wilson method* (www.wilsonlanguage.com/programs/wilson -reading-system), *Lindamood-Bell* (https://lindamoodbell.com), and *Fast Forward* (www.carnegielearning.com) are other reading programs that can be successful to teach reading skills.

- Sally Shaywitz's *Overcoming Dyslexia* (New York: Knopf, 2020) is an excellent resource for parents who are looking for proven ways to help their child with dyslexia. This book is also suitable for young adults and adults with dyslexia who are interested in learning more about their unique learning profiles. Sally Shaywitz is an internationally known doctor specializing in dyslexia.

- Interestingly, video game technology such as *Word Whomp* and action video games such as *Super Smash Bros.* have been shown to help children with dyslexia and improve their reading skills.[2] Of course, there are only specific programs that have been shown to be effective. Programs that improve visual attention and speed are particularly effective. *Tetris* is a game in which the player is required to manipulate designs. It is a good game to improve these skills.[3]

## Dyscalculia

- *Singapore Math* (www.singaporemath.com). Singapore math, rooted in the national curriculum of Singaporean schools for grades 1 through 6, emphasizes in-depth understanding of fewer math concepts through a three-step process: concrete, pictorial, and abstract. Developed in the 1980s, it prioritizes problem-solving and critical thinking skills, gaining global popularity in countries like the United States, Canada, and the United Kingdom. With its hands-on approach and focus on mastery, Singapore math is widely used in diverse educational settings worldwide.

- *Stern Structural Arithmetic* (https://sternmath.com). Stern Structural Arithmetic presents a holistic method for teaching fundamental math principles and building numerical intuition. Through hands-on, multisensory activities, students actively engage with mathematical concepts and patterns using vibrant blocks to represent numbers. The curriculum is carefully structured, guiding learners through a step-by-step journey from basic number understanding to proficiency in computation and problem-solving, fostering a deeper grasp of mathematics through interactive learning experiences.

- *Khan Academy* (www.khanacademy.org). Khan Academy offers a wide array of educational resources spanning various subjects and grade levels, making it a valuable tool for parents of students with learning differences. Its adaptive learning platform allows students to progress at their own pace, providing personalized instruction tailored to their individual needs. Additionally, it offers specialized content and resources specifically designed to support students with learning differences, empowering parents to supplement their child's education with targeted interventions and additional practice materials.
- *BBC Bitesize* (www.bbc.co.uk/bitesize). A free online resource supporting students aged three to sixteen and older with learning, revision, and homework, BBC Bitesize is written by teachers, and its lessons cater to diverse subjects and exam standards, aiding students in their academic preparation. It also fosters student well-being and offers career exploration opportunities, making it a valuable tool for learners worldwide.

### Dysgraphia

- *Handwriting without Tears* (www.lwtears.com/solutions/writing/handwriting-without-tears) is an excellent resource to help students write.
- *Occupational therapy* is recommended to strengthen pencil grip and improve legibility.

### Disorder of Written Expression

- Computer programs such as *Inspiration* and *Kidspiration* help with outlining.
- *Spell-check*, *Grammarly*, *speech-to-text*, and *ChatGPT* are all technologies that can help struggling writers.

### Autism

- Books such as Thomas Armstrong's *The Power of Neurodiversity* (Cambridge, MA: Da Capo Lifelong, 2010) and organizations such as *Autism Speaks* (www.autismspeaks.org) are resources that provide support.

- Global and Regional Asperger Syndrome Partnership (GRASP) is a global organization providing support for families.
- *NeuroTribes* by Steve Silberman (New York: Avery, 2015) is another wonderful book that illustrates both the disorder and resources for families.
- Therapy includes the *Greenspan Floortime Approach* (https://stanley greenspan.com), a program that encourages interaction with the autistic child. Briefly put, the therapist plays with the child, elaborating on the child's activity. For example, if the child is playing with cars by banging them together, the therapist helps the child interact in a more imaginative and connected manner.
- *ABA, or adaptive behavior analysis*, is the most widely used intervention with children with autism. An ABA therapist targets a goal behavior; for example, getting the child to communicate when he or she is hungry. The therapist then breaks down the behavior in segments and rewards the child every step of the way. Most young children with ASD get intensive ABA, as it has been proven to improve communication and interpersonal skills and reduce maladaptive behavior. There are many schools and programs that are entirely ABA based.
- *Play therapy*, *coaching*, *parent guidance*, and *support groups* are all useful treatment options for individuals with ASD and their families.

## ADD/ADHD

- *Driven to Distraction* by Edward M. Hallowell and John J. Ratey (New York: Vintage Books, 2011) is the bible of ADD and still very relevant. With this book, Hallowell emblazoned ADD on a national and global stage.
- *ADHD 2.0*, also by Edward M. Hallowell and John J. Ratey (New York: Ballantine Books, 2021), is the latest, updated, and extremely readable modern book that provides updated information and resources for families with ADHD.
- *Your Brain's Not Broken* by Tamara Rosier (Grand Rapids, MI: Revell, 2021) is a wonderful book that elaborates on how to understand ADD.

- Websites that explore the emotional impact of ADD and LD include the *Childmind Institute*, an organization rife with resources for parents of students with neurodivergence, and *CHADD*, a national organization designed to support parents with ADD children.
- Children with ADD often respond well to a combination of *medication*, such as stimulants, and *therapy* such as play therapy, behavior therapy, and group therapy. For those interested in this topic, *A Symphony of the Brain* by Jim Robbins (New York: Open Road + Grove/Atlantic, 2014) is an excellent book that describes the principles behind neurofeedback.

### Nonverbal Learning Disorders

- Sue Thompson wrote the bible on children with NVLD. Her book, *The Source for Nonverbal Learning Disorders* (Greenville, SC: LinguiSystems, 1997) introduces NVLD as a disorder and clarifies its far-reaching impact on children both academically and socially.
- *Executive function coaching* is often very useful for individuals with NVLD to help them with task completion and time management.

### Slowed Speed

- The book *Bright Kids Who Can't Keep Up*, by Ellen Braaten and Brian Willoughby (New York: Guilford Press, 2014), is a wonderful resource for those children who are highly intelligent but operate at a slower pace.

In sum, parenting and teaching a child with neurocognitive challenges is an all-consuming task that requires a great deal of understanding, patience, and information. I hope these resources get you on your way to finding the right support for both your child and you.

CHAPTER TEN

# FUTURE DIRECTIONS

What have we learned about parenting and teaching a child with neurocognitive challenges? As a neurocognitive psychologist with a deep passion for understanding and addressing neurocognitive challenges in children, my main focus revolves around empowering families and teachers with knowledge. I feel it's important to provide valuable insights into the intricacies of how children's brains are affected by neurocognitive disorders. By arming caregivers and educators with a comprehensive understanding of these challenges, we can collectively make a significant impact on their development. In this case, information about each disorder leads to critical intervention, helping children thrive and flourish academically, socially, and emotionally.

In this book, I've explained how to recognize and assess several different learning disorders and how to treat them. Each unique learning profile has its own strengths and weaknesses that need to be addressed. Children with attention deficit disorder (ADD) have trouble focusing; children with language-based learning disorders typically have difficulty with words and subjects such as reading and writing. Children with nonverbal learning disorders struggle when presented with visual information in subjects such as math and science. Last, children with autism spectrum disorder (ASD) don't understand emotions or social situations.

I created specific interventions geared to the challenges of each disorder. I elaborated on different types of therapy, classroom accommodations and modifications, and parenting strategies. The psychological and emotional impact of having a disability is significant, and I discussed how children typically feel about their disability; that is, embarrassed, frustrated, self-critical, and isolated. Parents also struggle with their feelings of concern for their children and experience real frustration regarding their own challenges and anxiety about how to parent them. I provided useful strategies and resources to help both children and their families cope with the fallout from the disorder.

I touched on special issues, such as the impact of COVID, and illuminated how many children with disabilities really suffered due to the isolation and disruption in routine. But there was also a silver lining: children felt more relaxed and had the opportunity to spend more time with their families. I provided resources for the families and also discussed how these disorders impact—both positively and negatively—the siblings of those with neurocognitive challenges. I highlighted cultural concerns, identified disorders across ethnicities, and pointed out the need for sensitivity regarding issues such as bilingualism. Last, I devoted a chapter on preparing children with neurocognitive challenges for college and how to support them best throughout their college years.

I proposed several principles essential to keep in mind when working with children with neurocognitive challenges. First, parents and professionals need to recognize that their academic, social, and emotional issues stem from "hardwiring" in the brain, not a lack of intelligence. Children with attention and learning challenges perceive the world very differently than neurotypical children, and thus their responses are skewed and often atypical. Recognizing the unique learning style of your child is the key to unlocking his or her potential.

Second, children are multidimensional; our responsibility is to be attuned to their distinctive strengths and talents and acknowledge the strategies they use to counterbalance or adapt to their disorders. My best recommendation is to help patients in compensating, modifying, adapting, and nurturing their abilities. It is crucial to recognize and celebrate the positive aspects that arise from their challenges, fostering an environment that not only supports their growth, but also helps them build a positive self-image. Through our guidance, we can instill a sense of pride and self-worth, encouraging them to embrace their uniqueness and navigate their journey with confidence!

Last, there are so many resources out there that can be helpful to children with neurocognitive challenges and their families. There is exciting and innovative research underway, promising improved assessment, intervention, and support for children with neurocognitive challenges. Our progress in recent decades is nothing short of remarkable, and the future holds even greater promise for the well-being of our exceptional children! Let's explore some upcoming research and intervention.

## FUTURE DIRECTIONS IN RESEARCH

### Neurobiology

There are promising imaging studies that have identified challenges in the brains of children with attention and learning disorders that help us understand their deficits better. For example, we see changes in the frontal lobe with individuals with attention deficit hyperactivity disorder (ADHD).[1] This finding makes sense, as the frontal lobe is responsible for organization, impulse control, and regulation.

A promising new direction in intervention is precision medicine, medical care that uses genetic profiling to customize medical care for specific patient groups and offer targeted interventions based on individual factors such as lifestyle, genetic markers, and symptoms. For example, ADHD can be effectively treated using precision medicine, taking into consideration associated symptoms such as sleep disturbances and irritability.[2] Furthermore, there have been remarkable advances in treating ASD with new medications to treat specific symptoms such as anxiety, sensory sensitivity, and rigidity.[3]

### Use of Computer Technology

We know that technological devices from keyboarding on laptops, setting alarms on smartphones, or making use of the plethora of computer programs available on the internet are technologies that can help our children with neurocognitive challenges, making their lives so much easier! We have also referenced the drawbacks of computers and technology; reliance on screens can lead to a full-blown screen addiction and mindless scrolling on the phone, all of which definitely exacerbate attention and social problems and negatively impact mental health. Although we celebrate new technologies, we also need to be careful when touting their benefits, to be aware of the pitfalls, and to make sure to help our children use technology responsibly.

Similarly, although use of technology has been touted as a revolutionary breakthrough in working with patients with ADD and ASD, there is no firm evidence that these programs are effective.[4] The premise is simple: computer programs give step-by-step directions, offer immediate feedback, and allow students to work at their own pace. Therefore, this type of instruction appears ideal for children with attention and learning difficulties. The students are actively involved with the material and hopefully enjoy the experience. However, these programs have not lived up to the hype that surrounded them. There is no substitute for personal interaction when helping children learn social and academic skills. Computer programs can help children with specific skills, but we must always monitor their usage to ensure their efficacy.

### Psychosocial Interventions

Psychosocial interventions are psychological treatments that focus on enhancing social and life skills. These therapies help improve time management, organization, social skills, and performance.[5] Particularly in late adolescence and during college, when individuals are very interested in their peers and benefit from learning skills with others, these treatments both educate and help empower them to leverage their strengths collectively. There are many effective psychosocial programs in college that can help students with learning and attention disorders. For example, Robert Manganello helped college students with language-based learning disorders improve their social skills by providing group intervention that was based on helping them make small talk and use language more effectively.[6] Students can also benefit from learning how to adapt to new environments and recognize social cues. Peer mentoring programs are extremely valuable to help educate students and improve interpersonal skills.

Collaboration among therapists, tutors, and educators is crucial to providing support. Psychosocial programs are also effective in every stage of child development, starting with preschool, since all children socialize in groups. There are many preschool programs that can help parents become more effective with their kids with neurocognitive challenges. In addition, there are behavior programs in the classroom that help teachers work with children with learning and attention difficulties, such as behavior charts and incentive systems. Further, peer interventions are fantastic for improving behaviors and social skills such as impulse control and flexibility, which are key elements to social and academic success.[7] As children with ASD greatly benefit from social skills training, more research in this area will help ascertain the best method of delivery of these services.

## Neurofeedback and Mindfulness

Biofeedback is an established treatment method that was originally used to reduce anxiety. Originally, a simple, galvanic skin response indicator, which is a measure of perspiration, was attached to the patient's finger to evaluate anxiety. For example, if a patient was phobic about dogs, the therapist would attach the indicator to the patient's finger. The patient would be shown a picture of a dog, and the skin indicator would then measure the sweaty palms that accompany anxiety. The therapist and patient would work together on relaxation techniques. Initially, the therapist would expose the patient to images of dogs and then eventually to a real dog, helping the patient master his or her fears.

From these humble beginnings, neurofeedback emerged into a more sophisticated intervention. Instead of measuring perspiration, brain wave activity is monitored via electrodes. We can tell from the brain wave activity if the patient is anxious, inattentive, alert, or relaxed. The patient then executes an activity on the computer using his or her brain wave activity only. For example, the goal of the program is to open a flower whose petals are closed. The program is coordinated with the patient's brain wave activity, so the flower opens only when the patient both focuses and relaxes. The patient learns how to put him- or herself in this state and then can transfer that skill to other situations. I refer to this technique as going to the "brain gym," because just as a visit to the gym strengthens your physical muscles, neurofeedback helps exercise your attention muscles, so your attention is stronger in class. This technique has been used for children with ADD and learning disorders. It is seen as a promising treatment, but more research needs to be conducted to determine its efficacy and usefulness.[8]

Mindfulness meditation is another technique focused on helping control mood and one's state of mind. Mindfulness is the practice of encouraging the state of "attending" to your body and your breath in order to put yourself in a relaxed and alert state.[9] The method has been shown to improve attention, reduce stress, and improve mood in those with ADHD.[10] One promising study taught mindfulness techniques to parents and children with very good results. The children's attention symptoms improved and the parents reported improved behaviors at home.[11]

## Inclusion

Recently, there has been a lot of discussion surrounding inclusion, which is including children with special needs in the mainstream classroom. Inclusion can range from placing neurodivergent children in a completely mainstream setting and offering them additional support, such as pull-out academic support services, or mainstreaming the children for the subjects in which they excel and keeping them in smaller classes for the subjects with which they have more difficulty. Another model places children with learning and attention challenges in a mainstream classroom with an additional special education teacher. This model is called ICT, integrative collaborative teaching, as it's a collaborative model and the mainstream teacher coordinates with the special education teacher on all aspects of the classroom. However, I must emphasize that there is no one-size-fits-all in this field of special education, and we must determine each student's unique needs. For example, there are students who greatly benefit from attending a special education school where every subject (including gym!) is geared for their learning needs. Other students do very well in a mainstream environment with an extra special education teacher in their class for support. Regardless of whether a student is placed in special ed or in a mainstream school, there must be an individualized learning plan in place tailored specifically to the student's goals, using best practices and current research to help the student succeed.

## STRATEGIES FOR LIVING WITH EACH DISORDER

I discussed how to support children with neurocognitive challenges at home, in the classroom, with peers, and emotionally. Living with a neurocognitive disorder is exhausting and just getting through the day can be extremely frustrating. Here are some "life hacks" that can really make a difference in your child's day-to-day life.

First, it is extremely important to stay positive and confident about your child's success. The more you can embrace your child's strengths and challenges as part of the unique package that makes up him or her, the better off you and your child will be! Reviewing the positive qualities of each disorder is key. I suggest creating affirmations for your child, writing them out, putting them in key places throughout the home, and making it a point to compliment your child whenever possible.

### Dr. Sorscher's Statements of Positive Regard

- I have a unique way of looking at the world.
- My energy is contagious.
- I am valuable.
- There is no one right way of doing things.
- I can do it, just give me time.
- I am smart.
- There is no such thing as being lazy.
- I will get to where I want to go.
- I can ask for help.
- My superpower is [fill in the blank—this could be empathy, diligence, humor, creativity, etc.].
- I am lovable.
- I know how to take care of myself.

## SELF-DISCLOSURE

Children, including those with neurocognitive challenges, benefit greatly from having role models to whom they can relate. When adults in their lives, such as parents or therapists, share their own struggles, it provides children with hope for a successful future. My esteemed supervisor, the wonderful Dr. Clarice Kestenbaum, emphasizes the importance of sharing similar stories to those of the child's struggle; she is so keen on this idea that she suggests inventing a story if there isn't a real story to convey! This practice helps children feel less isolated and more hopeful, knowing that someone they admire has faced similar challenges and overcome them. Sharing such stories fosters a sense of connection, hope, and empowerment. Importantly, it can instill a sense of resilience and belief in their own ability to conquer difficulties. I cannot stress how often I see the positive impact of this strategy.

To wrap up, I want to share that I am a member of the tribe. I have a learning disorder and my three children each have their own neurocognitive challenges. I was an academically capable child and a voracious reader who skipped second grade. Despite this, I was placed in a special math group with two of the lowest achieving students in my class. I recall struggling to memorize multiplication tables; I could not retain the basic tenets of mathematics, despite a nearly photographic memory. To this day, I often count on my fingers—a habit established in elementary school. I understand the pain, frustration, and embarrassment that comes from having widely variable skills. I also have a very difficult time reading maps, following geographic directions, or finding my way to where I'm going; I often take many wrong turns before finally arriving. I've grown so accustomed to getting lost that I factor in extra time for my trips. I even routinely get lost when traveling to and from places that I have been many times before, such as the grocery store and the library. These experiences can take their toll on those traveling with me. My son recently reflected on how stressful traveling with me was before the welcome advent of GPS.

My learning disorder can be hard for others to relate to or understand. In the past, it made me miserable as I struggled to explain to my parents, teachers, and friends my failures in math, with directions, and with learning to write in cursive. I felt ashamed and I retreated into the worlds of books and sports, where I flourished. The acute anxiety and bewilderment surrounding my inability to acquire skills and information, particularly when my peers appeared to do so effortlessly, took a deep emotional toll. I avoided math class, convinced I was simply "stupid" or "bad." I was finally able to approach the subject only when I studied for my graduate school entrance exams, but I still had significant gaps in my knowledge base dating back to my era of avoidance. These feelings of incompetence led to anxiety, depression, and low self-esteem.

It was not until my graduate school years that I realized I had a non-verbal learning disorder. Suddenly my learning challenges made sense. This discovery was a tremendous relief and gave me the power to advocate for myself. Interestingly, when I shared my diagnosis, it was met with disbelief. People said, "You can't have a learning disorder. You're too smart." I took these comments as an opportunity to educate others about learning disorders, explaining that these disabilities exist independent of perceived intelligence and impact intelligent people as much as anyone else. Eventually, I was able to come to terms with my learning disorder and the shame I experienced because of it. This involved confronting my frustration head-on and implementing and adhering to compensatory strategies that worked. I also learned to lighten up a bit about my learning disabilities. For instance, rather than getting upset when my assistant notices my poor handwriting, I'm able to share a laugh with him about it.

These experiences have informed my clinical and neuropsychological interventions with my patients. As I began to assess and treat patients with learning and attention disorders, I realized my history was an asset; I can both sympathize and empathize with the frustrations that arise when bright students face neurocognitive challenges, and I can use self-disclosure as a tool while helping patients grapple with their specific challenges. Drawing from my own experience, I'm able to creatively devise individualized strategies to cope with their feelings of frustration, shame, sadness, and anxiety. This typically involves encouraging patients to express pride in their accomplishments while concurrently helping them understand the impact of their disability.

It's so meaningful and important to understand the complexities of your child's neurocognitive challenge; it's truly essential to help him or her flourish and thrive academically, socially, and emotionally. I wish you all the best on this exhilarating and often exhausting job of parenting and teaching our neurodivergent children. And I applaud you for doing so. As a fellow patient, parent, and therapist, our children are lucky to live in a world sophisticated and open about their challenges. Let's continue to pave the way for them to lead incredible lives.

# NOTES

## CHAPTER ONE

1. National Center for Learning Disabilities, www.ncld.org, accessed May 1, 2024.

2. Sameule Cortese, Eric Konofal, Nigel Yateman, Marie-Christine Mouren, and Michel Lecendreux, "Sleep and Alertness in Children with Attention-Deficit/ Hyperactivity Disorder: A Systematic Review of the Literature," *Sleep* 29, no. 4 (2006): 504–11.

3. Donna Geffner and Deborah Ross-Swain, *Auditory Processing Disorders: Assessment, Management, and Treatment* (San Diego, CA: Plural Publishing, 2019).

## CHAPTER TWO

1. Bruce F. Pennington and Dorothy V. M. Bishop, "Relations among Speech, Language, and Reading Disorders," *Annual Review of Psychology* 60, no. 1 (2009): 283–306, https://doi.org/10.1146/annurev.psych.60.110707.163548.

2. Matthew J. Maenner et al., "Prevalence and Characteristics of Autism Spectrum Disorder among Children Aged 8 Years—Autism and Developmental Disabilities Monitoring Network, 11 Sites, United States, 2018," *Morbidity and Mortality Weekly Report: Surveillance Summaries* 70, no. 11 (December 2021): 1–16, https://doi.org/10.15585/mmwr.ss7011a1.

3. Lynda J. Katz, Gerald Goldstein, and Sue R. Beers, *Learning Disabilities in Older Adolescents and Adults: Clinical Utility of the Neuropsychological Perspective*, Critical Issues in Neuropsychology (New York: Springer, 2001), https://doi.org /10.1007/b108001.

4. Clare S. Allely, "Pain Sensitivity and Observer Perception of Pain in Individuals with Autistic Spectrum Disorder," *The Scientific World Journal* 2013, (2013): 1–20, 916178, https://doi.org/10.1155/2013/916178; Jaak Panksepp, "A Neurochemical Theory of Autism," *Trends in Neurosciences* 2 (1979): 174–77, https://doi.org/10.1016/0166-2236(79)90071-7; Tony L. Sahley and Jaak Panksepp, "Brain Opioids and Autism: An Updated Analysis of Possible Linkages," *Journal of Autism and Developmental Disorders* 17, no. 2 (1987): 201–16, https://doi .org/10.1007/bf01495056.

5. *Merriam-Webster*, s.v. "savant (*n.*)," www.merriam-webster.com/word-of -the-day/savant-2023-01-31, accessed February 18, 2024.

## CHAPTER THREE

1. M. S. Thambirajah and Lalitha Lakshmi Ramanujan, *Essentials of Learning Disabilities and Other Developmental Disorders* (New Delhi: Sage, 2016).

2. David Wechsler, *Wechsler Individual Achievement Test (WIAT-4)*, 4th ed. (San Antonio, TX: Pearson, 2020).

3. J. Lee Wiederholt and Brian R. Bryant, *Gray Oral Reading Test*, 5th ed. (Austin, TX: Pro-Ed, 2012).

4. Donald D. Hammill and Stephen C. Larsen, *Test of Written Language*, 3rd ed. (Los Angeles: Western Psychological Services, 1996).

5. Morrison F. Gardner, *Expressive One-Word Picture Vocabulary Test* (Novato, CA: Academic Therapy Publications, 2000).

6. Elisabeth H. Wiig, Eleanor Semel, and Wayne A. Secord, *Clinical Evaluation of Language Fundamentals*, 5th ed. (Bloomington, MN: Pearson, 2013).

7. Wayne Adams and David Sheslow, *Wide Range Assessment of Memory and Learning*, 3rd ed. (New York: Springer Link, 2021).

8. C. Keith Conners, *Conners Continuous Performance Test*, 3rd ed. (North Tonawanda, NY: Multi-Health Systems, 1995).

9. Susan K. Kongs, Laetitia L. Thompson, Grant L. Iverson, and Robert K. Heaton, *Wisconsin Card Sorting Test—64 Card Version* (Odessa, FL: Psychological Assessment Resources, 2000); Federica Scarpina and Sofia Tagini, "The Stroop Color and Word Test," *Frontiers in Psychology* 8, no. 557 (2017), https://doi.org/10.3389/fpsyg.2017.00557.

10. Robert W. Keith, *SCAN-C: Test for Auditory Processing Disorders in Children* (San Antonio, TX: The Psychological Corporation, 2000).

11. Katherine Gotham, Susan Risi, Andrew Pickles, and Catherine Lord, "The Autism Diagnostic Observation Schedule: Revised Algorithms for Diagnostic Validity," *Journal of Autism and Developmental Disorders* 37, no. 4 (April 2007): 613–27, https://doi.org/10.1007/s10803-006-0280-1.

12. Cecil R. Reynolds and Randy W. Kamphaus, *Behavior Assessment System for Children*, 3rd ed. (Bloomington, MN: Pearson, 2020).

13. John N. Constantino, *Social Responsiveness Scale*, 2nd ed. (Torrance, CA: Western Psychological Services, 2012).

## CHAPTER FIVE

1. Tamara McClintock Greenberg, *Psychodynamic Perspectives on Aging and Illness*, 2nd ed. (Cham, Switzerland: Springer, 2016).

## CHAPTER SIX

1. Mitchell L. Yell, Antonis Katsiyannis, Joseph B. Ryan, Kimberly A. McDuffie, and Lindsay Mattocks, "Ensure Compliance with the Individuals with

Disabilities Education Improvement Act of 2004," *Interventions in School and Clinic* 44, no. 1 (2008): 45–51, https://doi.org/10.1177/1053451208318875.

2. S. Hatcher and Angela M. Waguespack, "Academic Accommodations for Students with Disabilities," in *Helping Children at Home and School II: Handouts for Families and Educators*, ed. Andrea S. Canter, Leslie Z. Paige, Mark D. Roth, Ivonne Romero, and Servio A. Carroll (Bethesda, MD: National Association for School Psychologists, 2004).

3. Alexander Gantman, Steven K. Kapp, Kaely Orenski, and Elizabeth A. Laugeson, "Social Skills Training for Young Adults with High Functioning Autism Spectrum Disorder: A Randomized Control Pilot Study," *Journal of Autism and Developmental Disorders* 42, no. 6 (2012): 1094–1103, http://dx.doi.org/10.1007/s10803-011-1350-6.

## CHAPTER EIGHT

1. Erik H. Erikson, *Childhood and Society* (New York: W. W. Norton, 1950).

2. Marsha H. Levy-Warren, *The Adolescent Journey: Development, Identity Formation, and Psychotherapy* (Lanham, MD: Jason Aronson, 1996).

## CHAPTER NINE

1. Alison McCullough, "Viability and Effectiveness of Teletherapy for Pre-School Children with Special Needs," *International Journal of Language & Communication Disorders* 36, no. S1 (April 2001): 321–26, https://doi.org/10.3109/13682820109177905; Yuet Juhn Tse, Carolyn A. McCarty, Ann Vander Stoep, and Kathleen M. Myers, "Teletherapy Delivery of Caregiver Behavior Training for Children with Attention-Deficit Hyperactivity Disorder," *Telemedicine Journal and E-Health: The Official Journal of the American Telemedicine Association* 21, no. 6 (2015): 451–58, https://doi.org/10.1089/tmj.2014.0132.

2. Pogo Games, *Word Whomp HD* (Pogo Games, 2024); Masahiro Sakurai, *Super Smash Bros.* (Nintendo, 1999).

3. Alexey Pajitnov, *Tetris* (Sega, 1984).

## CHAPTER TEN

1. George Bush, "Cingulate, Frontal, and Parietal Cortical Dysfunction in Attention-Deficit/Hyperactivity Disorder," *Biological Psychiatry* 69, no. 12 (2011): 1160–67, https://doi.org/10.1016/j.biopsych.2011.01.022.

2. Evdokia Anagnostou, "Clinical Trials in Autism Spectrum Disorder: Evidence, Challenges, and Future Directions," *Current Opinion in Neurology* 31, no. 2 (April 2018): 119–25, https://doi.org/10.1097/wco.0000000000000542.

3. Cara R. Damiano, Carla A. Mazefsky, Susan W. White, and Gabriel S. Dichter, "Future Directions for Research in Autism Spectrum Disorders," *Journal of Clinical Child & Adolescent Psychology* 43, no. 5 (2014): 828–43, https://doi.org /10.1080/15374416.2014.945214; Johnny L. Matson and Rachel L. Goldin, "Comorbidity and Autism: Trends, Topics and Future Directions," *Research in Autism Spectrum Disorders* 7, no. 10 (October 2013): 1228–33, https://doi.org/10.1016/j .rasd.2013.07.003.

4. Cori More, "Digital Stories Targeting Social Skills for Children with Disabilities," *Intervention in School and Clinic* 43, no. 3 (2008): 168–77, https://doi .org/10.1177/1053451207312919; Laura Jiménez-Muñoz, Inmaculada Peñuelas-Calvo, Pilar Calvo-Rivera, Isaac Díaz-Oliván, Manon Moreno, Enrique Baca-García, and Alejandro Porras-Segovia, "Video Games for the Treatment of Autism Spectrum Disorder: A Systematic Review," *Journal of Autism and Developmental Disorders* 52, no. 1 (2021): 169–88, https://doi.org/10.1007/s10803-021-04934-9.

5. Margaret Weiss, Lily Trokenberg-Hechtman, and Gabrielle Weiss, *ADHD in Adulthood: A Guide to Current Theory, Diagnosis, and Treatment* (Baltimore: Johns Hopkins University Press, 1999); Brandon K. Schultz, Steven W. Evans, Joshua M. Langberg, and Alexander M. Schoemann, "Outcomes for Adolescents Who Comply with Long-Term Psychosocial Treatment for ADHD," *Journal of Consulting and Clinical Psychology* 85, no. 3 (March 2017): 250–61, https://doi .org/10.1037/ccp0000172; John J. Ratey, Mark S. Greenberg, Jules R. Bemporad, and Karen J. Lindem, "Unrecognized Attention-Deficit Hyperactivity Disorder in Adults Presenting for Outpatient Psychotherapy," *Journal of Child and Adolescent Psychopharmacology* 2, no. 4 (1992): 267–75, https://doi.org/10.1089 /cap.1992.2.267.

6. Robert E. Manganello, "Psychosocial Problems among Learning Disabled College Students," *Research and Teaching in Developmental Education* 9, no. 1 (Fall 1992): 67–78.

7. J. Russell Ramsay and Anthony L. Rostain, "Psychosocial Treatments for Attention-Deficit/Hyperactivity Disorder in Adults: Current Evidence and Future Directions," *Professional Psychology: Research and Practice* 38, no. 4 (August 2007): 338–46, https://doi.org/10.1037/0735-7028.38.4.338.

8. Abhishek Uday Patil, Deepa Madathil, Yang-Tang Fan, Ovid J. L. Tzeng, Chih-Mao Huang, and Hsu-Wen Huang, "Neurofeedback for the Education of Children with ADHD and Specific Learning Disorders: A Review," *Brain Sciences* 12, no. 9 (2022): 1238, https://doi.org/10.3390/brainsci12091238.

9. Chunzhen Xu, Robert Reid, and Allen Steckelberg, "Technology Applications for Children with ADHD: Assessing the Empirical Support," *Education and Treatment of Children* 25, no. 2 (May 2002): 224–48.

10. John T. Mitchell, Lidia Zylowska, and Scott H. Kollins, "Mindfulness Meditation Training for Attention-Deficit/Hyperactivity Disorder in Adulthood: Current Empirical Support, Treatment Overview, and Future Directions," *Cognitive and Behavioral Practice* 22, no. 2 (May 2015): 172–91, https://doi.org/10.1016/j.cbpra.2014.10.002.

11. Lidia Zylowska, Deborah L. Ackerman, May H. Yang, Julie L. Futrell, Nancy L. Horton, T. Sigi Hale, Caroly Pataki, and Susan L. Smalley, "Mindfulness Meditation Training in Adults and Adolescents with ADHD," *Journal of Attention Disorders* 11, no. 6 (2007): 737–46, https://doi.org/10.1177/1087054707308502.

# BIBLIOGRAPHY

Adams, Wayne, and David Sheslow. *Wide Range Assessment of Memory and Learning*. 3rd ed. New York: Springer Link, 2021.

Allely, Clare S. "Pain Sensitivity and Observer Perception of Pain in Individuals with Autistic Spectrum Disorder." *The Scientific World Journal* (2013): 1–20. https://doi.org/10.1155/2013/916178.

Anagnostou, Evdokia. "Clinical Trials in Autism Spectrum Disorder: Evidence, Challenges, and Future Directions." *Current Opinion in Neurology* 31, no. 2 (April 2018): 119–25. https://doi.org/10.1097/wco.0000000000000542.

Armstrong, Thomas. *The Power of Neurodiversity: Unleashing the Advantages of Your Differently Wired Brain*. Cambridge, MA: Da Capo Lifelong, 2010.

Braaten, Ellen, and Brian Willoughby. *Bright Kids Who Can't Keep Up: Help Your Child Overcome Slow Processing Speed and Succeed in a Fast-Paced World*. New York: Guilford Press, 2014.

Bush, George. "Cingulate, Frontal, and Parietal Cortical Dysfunction in Attention-Deficit/Hyperactivity Disorder." *Biological Psychiatry* 69, no. 12 (2011): 1160–67. https://doi.org/10.1016/j.biopsych.2011.01.022.

Conners, C. Keith. *Conners Continuous Performance Test*. 3rd ed. North Tonawanda, NY: Multi-Health Systems, 1995.

Constantino, John N. *Social Responsiveness Scale*. 2nd ed. Torrance, CA: Western Psychological Services, 2012.

Cortese, Samuele, Eric Konofal, Nigel Yateman, Marie-Christine Mouren, and Michel Lecendreux. "Sleep and Alertness in Children with Attention-Deficit/Hyperactivity Disorder: A Systematic Review of the Literature." *Sleep* 29, no. 4 (2006): 504–11.

Damiano, Cara R., Carla A. Mazefsky, Susan W. White, and Gabriel S. Dichter. "Future Directions for Research in Autism Spectrum Disorders." *Journal of Clinical Child & Adolescent Psychology* 43, no. 5 (2014): 828–43. https://doi.org/10.1080/15374416.2014.945214.

Erikson, Erik H. *Childhood and Society*. New York: W. W. Norton, 1950.

Gantman, Alexander, Steven K. Kapp, Kaely Orenski, and Elizabeth A. Laugeson. "Social Skills Training for Young Adults with High Functioning Autism Spectrum Disorder: A Randomized Control Pilot Study." *Journal of Autism and Developmental Disorders* 42, no. 6 (2012): 1094–1103. http://dx.doi.org/10.1007/s10803-011-1350-6.

Gardner, Morrison F. *Expressive One-Word Picture Vocabulary Test.* Novato, CA: Academic Therapy Publications, 2000.

Geffner, Donna, and Deborah Ross-Swain. *Auditory Processing Disorders: Assessment, Management, and Treatment.* 3rd ed. San Diego, CA: Plural Publishing, 2019.

Gotham, Katherine, Susan Risi, Andrew Pickles, and Catherine Lord. "The Autism Diagnostic Observation Schedule: Revised Algorithms for Diagnostic Validity." *Journal of Autism and Developmental Disorders* 37, no. 4 (April 2007): 613–27. https://doi.org/10.1007/s10803-006-0280-1.

Greenberg, Tamara McClintock. *Psychodynamic Perspectives on Aging and Illness.* 2nd ed. Cham, Switzerland: Springer, 2016.

Greenspan Floortime Approach. "What Is the Greenspan Floortime Approach?" https://stanleygreenspan.com/. Accessed January 8, 2024.

Hallowell, Edward M., and John J. Ratey. *ADHD 2.0: New Science and Essential Strategies for Thriving with Distraction—From Childhood through Adulthood.* New York: Ballantine Books, 2021.

———. *Driven to Distraction: Recognizing and Coping with Attention Deficit Disorder from Childhood through Adulthood.* Rev. ed. New York: Vintage Books, 2011.

Hammill, Donald D., and Stephen C. Larsen. *Test of Written Language.* 3rd ed. Los Angeles: Western Psychological Services, 1996.

Hatcher, S., and Angela M. Waguespack. "Academic Accommodations for Students with Disabilities." In *Helping Children at Home and School II: Handouts for Families and Educators.* Edited by Andrea S. Canter, Leslie Z. Paige, Mark D. Roth, Ivonne Romero, and Servio A. Carroll. Bethesda, MD: National Association for School Psychologists, 2004.

Jiménez-Muñoz, Laura, Inmaculada Peñuelas-Calvo, Pilar Calvo-Rivera, Isaac Díaz-Oliván, Manon Moreno, Enrique Baca-García, and Alejandro Porras-Segovia. "Video Games for the Treatment of Autism Spectrum Disorder: A Systematic Review." *Journal of Autism and Developmental Disorders* 52, no. 1 (2021): 169–88. https://doi.org/10.1007/s10803-021-04934-9.

Katz, Lynda J., Gerald Goldstein, and Sue R. Beers. *Learning Disabilities in Older Adolescents and Adults: Clinical Utility of the Neuropsychological Perspective.* Critical Issues in Neuropsychology. New York: Springer, 2001. https://doi.org/10.1007/b108001.

Keith, Robert W. *SCAN-C: Test for Auditory Processing Disorders in Children.* San Antonio, TX: The Psychological Corporation, 2000.

Kongs, Susan K., Laetitia L. Thompson, Grant L. Iverson, and Robert K. Heaton. *Wisconsin Card Sorting Test—64 Card Version.* Odessa, FL: Psychological Assessment Resources, 2000.

Levy-Warren, Marsha H. *The Adolescent Journey: Development, Identity Formation, and Psychotherapy.* Lanham, MD: Jason Aronson, 1996.

Maenner, Matthew J., Kelly A. Shaw, Amanda V. Bakian, Deborah A. Bilder, Maureen S. Durkin, Amy Esler, Sarah M. Furnier, Libby Hallas, Jennifer

Hall-Lande, Allison Hudson, Michelle M. Hughes, Mary Patrick, Karen Pierce, Jenny N. Poynter, Angelica Salinas, Josephine Shenouda, Alison Vehorn, Zachary Warren, John N. Constantino, Monica DiRienzo, Robert T. Fitzgerald, Andrea Grzybowski, Margaret H. Spivey, Sydney Pettygrove, Walter Zahorodny, Akilah Ali, Jennifer G. Andrews, Thaer Baroud, Johanna Gutierrez, Amy Hewitt, Li-Ching Lee, Maya Lopez, Kristen Clancy Mancilla, Dedria McArthur, Yvette D. Schwenk, Anita Washington, Susan Williams, and Mary E. Cogswell. "Prevalence and Characteristics of Autism Spectrum Disorder among Children Aged 8 Years—Autism and Developmental Disabilities Monitoring Network, 11 Sites, United States, 2018." *Morbidity and Mortality Weekly Report: Surveillance Summaries* 70, no. 11 (December 2021): 1–16. https://doi.org/10.15585/mmwr.ss7011a1.

Manganello, Robert E. "Psychosocial Problems among Learning Disabled College Students." *Research and Teaching in Developmental Education* 9, no. 1 (Fall 1992): 67–78.

Matson, Johnny L., and Rachel L. Goldin. "Comorbidity and Autism: Trends, Topics and Future Directions." *Research in Autism Spectrum Disorders* 7, no. 10 (October 2013): 1228–33. https://doi.org/10.1016/j.rasd.2013.07.003.

McCullough, Alison. "Viability and Effectiveness of Teletherapy for Pre-School Children with Special Needs." *International Journal of Language & Communication Disorders* 36, no. S1 (April 2001): 321–26. https://doi.org/10.3109/13682820109177905.

Mitchell, John T., Lidia Zylowska, and Scott H. Kollins. "Mindfulness Meditation Training for Attention-Deficit/Hyperactivity Disorder in Adulthood: Current Empirical Support, Treatment Overview, and Future Directions." *Cognitive and Behavioral Practice* 22, no. 2 (May 2015): 172–91. https://doi.org/10.1016/j.cbpra.2014.10.002.

More, Cori. "Digital Stories Targeting Social Skills for Children with Disabilities." *Intervention in School and Clinic* 43, no. 3 (2008): 168–77. https://doi.org/10.1177/1053451207312919.

Pajitnov, Alexey. *Tetris*. Sega, 1984.

Panksepp, Jaak. "A Neurochemical Theory of Autism." *Trends in Neurosciences* 2 (1979): 174–77. https://doi.org/10.1016/0166-2236(79)90071-7.

Patil, Abhishek Uday, Deepa Madathil, Yang-Tang Fan, Ovid J. L. Tzeng, Chih-Mao Huang, and Hsu-Wen Huang. "Neurofeedback for the Education of Children with ADHD and Specific Learning Disorders: A Review." *Brain Sciences* 12, no. 9 (2022): 1238. https://doi.org/10.3390/brainsci12091238.

Pennington, Bruce F., and Dorothy V. M. Bishop. "Relations among Speech, Language, and Reading Disorders." *Annual Review of Psychology* 60, no. 1 (2009): 283–306. https://doi.org/10.1146/annurev.psych.60.110707.163548.

Pogo Games. *Word Whomp HD*. Pogo Games, 2024.

Ramsay, J. Russell, and Anthony L. Rostain. "Psychosocial Treatments for Attention-Deficit/Hyperactivity Disorder in Adults: Current Evidence and Future Directions." *Professional Psychology: Research and Practice* 38, no. 4 (August 2007): 338–46. https://doi.org/10.1037/0735-7028.38.4.338.

Ratey, John J., Mark S. Greenberg, Jules R. Bemporad, and Karen J. Lindem. "Unrecognized Attention-Deficit Hyperactivity Disorder in Adults Presenting for Outpatient Psychotherapy." *Journal of Child and Adolescent Psychopharmacology* 2, no. 4 (1992): 267–75. https://doi.org/10.1089/cap.1992.2.267.

Reynolds, Cecil R., and Randy W. Kamphaus. *Behavior Assessment System for Children*. 3rd ed. Bloomington, MN: Pearson, 2020.

Robbins, Jim. *A Symphony in the Brain: The Evolution of the New Brain Wave Biofeedback*. Rev. ed. New York: Open Road + Grove/Atlantic, 2014. Kindle.

Rosier, Tamara. *Your Brain's Not Broken: Strategies for Navigating Your Emotions and Life with ADHD*. Grand Rapids, MI: Revell, 2021.

Sahley, Tony L., and Jaak Panksepp. "Brain Opioids and Autism: An Updated Analysis of Possible Linkages." *Journal of Autism and Developmental Disorders* 17, no. 2 (1987): 201–16. https://doi.org/10.1007/bf01495056.

Sakurai, Masahiro. *Super Smash Bros*. Nintendo, 1999.

Scarpina, Federica, and Sofia Tagini. "The Stroop Color and Word Test." *Frontiers in Psychology* 8, no. 557 (2017). https://doi.org/10.3389/fpsyg.2017.00557.

Schultz, Brandon K., Steven W. Evans, Joshua M. Langberg, and Alexander M. Schoemann. "Outcomes for Adolescents Who Comply with Long-Term Psychosocial Treatment for ADHD." *Journal of Consulting and Clinical Psychology* 85, no. 3 (March 2017), 250–61. https://doi.org/10.1037/ccp0000172.

Silberman, Steve. *NeuroTribes: The Legacy of Autism and the Future of Neurodiversity*. New York: Avery, 2015.

Thambirajah, M. S., and Lalitha Lakshmi Ramanujan. *Essentials of Learning Disabilities and Other Developmental Disorders*. New Delhi: Sage, 2016.

Thompson, Sue. *The Source for Nonverbal Learning Disorders*. Greenville, SC: LinguiSystems, 1997.

Tse, Yuet Juhn, Carolyn A. McCarty, Ann Vander Stoep, and Kathleen M. Myers. "Teletherapy Delivery of Caregiver Behavior Training for Children with Attention-Deficit Hyperactivity Disorder." *Telemedicine Journal and E-Health: The Official Journal of the American Telemedicine Association* 21, no. 6 (2015): 451–58. https://doi.org/10.1089/tmj.2014.0132.

Wechsler, David. *Wechsler Individual Achievement Test (WIAT-4)*. 4th ed. San Antonio: Pearson, 2020.

Weiss, Margaret, Lily Trokenberg Hechtman, and Gabrielle Weiss. *ADHD in Adulthood: A Guide to Current Theory, Diagnosis, and Treatment*. Baltimore: Johns Hopkins University Press, 1999.

Wiederholt, J. Lee, and Brian R. Bryant. *Gray Oral Reading Test*. 5th ed. Austin, TX: Pro-Ed, 2012.

Wiig, Elisabeth H., Eleanor Semel, and Wayne A. Secord. *Clinical Evaluation of Language Fundamentals*. 5th ed. Bloomington, MN: Pearson, 2013.

Xu, Chunzhen, Robert Reid, and Allen Steckelberg. "Technology Applications for Children with ADHD: Assessing the Empirical Support." *Education and Treatment of Children* 25, no. 2 (May 2002): 224–48.

Yell, Mitchell L., Antonis Katsiyannis, Joseph B. Ryan, Kimberly A. McDuffie, and Lindsay Mattocks. "Ensure Compliance with the Individuals with Disabilities Education Improvement Act of 2004." *Interventions in School and Clinic* 44, no. 1 (2008): 45–51. https://doi.org/10.1177/1053451208318875.

Zylowska, Lidia, Deborah L. Ackerman, May H. Yang, Julie L. Futrell, Nancy L. Horton, T. Sigi Hale, Caroly Pataki, and Susan L. Smalley. "Mindfulness Meditation Training in Adults and Adolescents with ADHD." *Journal of Attention Disorders* 11, no. 6 (2007): 737–46. https://doi.org/10.1177/1087054707308502.

# INDEX

# ABOUT THE AUTHOR

**Dr. Nechama Sorscher** is a clinical psychologist and neuropsychologist who maintains a private practice in New York City's Upper West Side, specializing in assessing and treating patients with learning and attention difficulties. Dr. Sorscher graduated with a PhD in clinical psychology from Adelphi University and has a certificate in psychotherapy and psychoanalysis from NYU's postdoctoral program. She has published scholarly articles and book chapters on learning and attention difficulties as well as on trauma and child development. Additionally, Dr. Sorscher supervises and teaches psychological assessment at the William Alanson White Institute. She enjoys conducting individual and group psychotherapy and regularly provides parent guidance and school consultations related to learning disorders and behavioral functioning.

www.ingramcontent.com/pod-product-compliance
Lightning Source LLC
Chambersburg PA
CBHW031547260326
41914CB00002B/309

* 9 7 8 1 5 3 8 1 9 2 1 3 9 *